HOW TO START YOUR OWN BUSINESS

D0170872

Edited by William D. Putt

247220

This book was set in CRT Baskerville,
printed on R&E Book,
and bound in Columbia Millbank Vellum-4321
by The Colonial Press Inc.
in the United States of America.

Library of Congress Cataloging in Publication Data

Putt, William D.
  How to start your own business.

  An outgrowth of a series of seminars held by the MIT Alumni Association.
  Bibliography: p.
  1. Business—Addresses, essays, lectures. 2. Business enterprises—Addresses,
essays, lectures. 3. Entrepreneur—Addresses, essays, lectures. I. Massachusetts
Institure of Technology. Alumni Association. II. Title.
  HF5353.P87   658.1'141   74-6120
  ISBN 0-262-16060-9

HOW TO START YOUR OWN BUSINESS

The Alumni Association of the
Massachusetts Institute of Technology

Distributed by The MIT Press
Cambridge, Massachusetts, and London, England

CONTENTS

FOREWORD*

This book grows in many ways from a base of M.I.T. entrepreneurship: the entrepreneurial spirit and demands of M.I.T. alumni called into being the nationwide series of alumni seminars that led to this work; M.I.T. entrepreneurial spin-offs were the source of most of the data for my own extensive research into entrepreneurship; and M.I.T. alumni entrepreneurs are largely responsible for organizing and writing the various chapters of this volume.

It may be fitting to review briefly some of what we know about M.I.T.-based entrepreneurs stemming from the research that I have done since 1964 with the aid of numerous graduate student assistants. Over a period of several years we gathered data on nearly 300 new companies, most of them technically oriented, and over half formed by entrepreneurs who had previously worked for an M.I.T. laboratory or academic department. Table 1 indicates the organizational sources of the new enterprises we investigated. It is important to note that this research by no means covers M.I.T. entrepreneurship completely—it merely samples it in reasonable depth.

In our research we have examined how these new companies have effectively utilized advanced technology; we have studied

* My thanks to *Technology Review* for permission to quote extensively from my article "How to Succeed in a New Technology Enterprise," *Technology Review*, Vol. 73, No. 2 (Dec. 1970)—Edward B. Roberts.

Table 1. Sources of New Enterprises Investigated

Sources	Number of Companies Studied
M.I.T. laboratories:	
Electronic Systems Laboratory	11
Instrumentation (now Draper) Laboratory	30
Lincoln Laboratory	50
Research Laboratory for Electronics	14
	105
M.I.T. academic departments:	
Aeronautics and Astronautics	18
Chemical Engineering (Ph.D.'s)	18
Electrical Engineering	15
Mechanical Engineering	10
Metallurgy	8
	69
Government research laboratory	16
Not-for-profit systems engineering organization	5
Industrial electronic systems contractor	39
Special studies:	
Computer firms in Boston	16
Consumer-oriented manufacturers	46
Total companies studied	296

the backgrounds and psychological characteristics of the entrepreneurs; we have looked into the marketing processes and organizational patterns of the new firms; and we have considered the decision-making processes of venture capital organizations and how these and other venture capital problems (including the decision to "go public") have affected the success of new technical companies.

What are the characteristics of the men who formed these companies? The entrepreneurs are indeed an intriguing lot, and in examining them we are struck by several key characteristics. To report them is not to say that every entrepreneur must have these characteristics to be successful, but the reader may indeed wish to compare himself and his associates with these prototypes in considering whether starting a new business is going to be suited to his personal makeup.

The first characteristic of the entrepreneurs that we note involves their family background. In all the samples studied, about 50 percent of the entrepreneurs came from homes in which the father was self-employed. The likely rationale may be put this way: if your father was in business for himself, you have probably been exposed to a background of business conversations in the home; whether you realize it or not, you tend to think in business terms more than others without such exposure; you identify with the vocabulary and concepts of entrepreneurship—employees, suppliers, pricing, profit, and cash flow. This is not to say that such a background is essential, but we think that this kind of entrepreneurial heritage is an important force that tends to push people toward starting new businesses.

Our evidence suggests that would-be entrepreneurs would do well to ask themselves some questions: Do I really have a long-term familiarity with business considerations? Am I acclimated to the type of thinking and life associated with running my own business? Is it a way of life and kind of responsibility I will enjoy? Those who come from a home in which the father was in business for himself probably have a better understanding of whether this kind of life is for them.

The second notable common feature of the entrepreneurs is age: the average entrepreneur coming from an M.I.T. laboratory was thirty-one or thirty-two at the time of starting his company. (But it is important to note that these data pertain to companies formed typically in 1961 or 1962. I am convinced by observing the current scene that the age of entrepreneurship is indeed going down, and this trend is probably going to continue.) In fact, very few entrepreneurs are over forty at the time of company initiation. The relative youth of the entrepreneur seems significant in two ways.

The older a person is, the greater is his commitment to established patterns of activity—family, organization, outside activities, community—and the greater the difficulty in breaking those patterns. Not only are there psychological difficulties, but there are also likely to be meaningful entanglements and relationships with others. Breaking these associations may pose costs very much greater than any possible reward. There are exceptions to the general pattern of youth: for example, two companies we studied were formed by M.I.T. professors who had reached the age of sixty-five and were put on retirement status; both companies were successful.

The point to be made in writing about these two exceptions at age sixty-five is not simply to say that a few entrepreneurs were not young, but rather to argue for the second characteristic of youth: vigor and energy. To start a company and get it under way requires a tremendous amount of energy and effort on the part of the entrepreneur. These abilities are usually characteristic of younger people—but not always. When we speak of the typical youth of entrepreneurs, what we really interpret our data as saying is that successful entrepreneurs are people who are willing to break out of the entanglements of their present situations. They are able to commit generous amounts of their time, effort, and energy to starting a new enterprise. (That commitment of time, effort, and energy will almost surely be at the expense of many other activities, including particularly the entrepreneur's family; indeed, this competition with family for energy, attention, and devotion to a new organization is one of the problems that arises in many new firms. The new enterprise can become a taxing mistress.)

A third characteristic of the entrepreneur is his education. Our studies included primarily entrepreneurs who left advanced technology organizations; so technical education itself is expected. But it is significant that the typical entrepreneur we examined had a master's degree—usually in engineering, sometimes in science, occasionally in other fields—and had in fact gone somewhat beyond the master's degree by taking several additional courses. We had entrepreneurs with doctorates in our sample, and we had others with only bachelor's degrees and even some without college degrees. But the master's seemed to be the most specific symbol of participation in advanced and advancing technologies.

The entrepreneur was not necessarily a technical genius; he was not necessarily the inventive mind behind the company; he was not necessarily the man who came up with the brilliant technical advances himself. But our studies suggest that if the basis of the company is technical—if the new enterprise is working at the forefront of a technology—then its founder probably should have sufficient background through education and experience to participate actively in that technology, to understand the work and contributions of others in that field, and to put developments in the marketplace in their proper context in relation to the advancing technology. The master's degree simply represents an appropriate degree of understanding and background.

A fourth characteristic of the entrepreneur is suggested by our finding that entrepreneurs usually have come out of development rather than research activity. This is important in terms of which people are suited for entrepreneurship and make effective entrepreneurs. The development process, in contrast to research, involves translating ideas and skills into some form of utilization—hardware, production, whatever the actual specific objective. In contrast, research is a process of the creation or enlargement of knowledge. Entrepreneurship is in fact more akin to development—to applying skills and knowledge to create something that is real and is clearly useful. The man who has been working in development activities has already come closer to the things expected of him as an entrepreneur than has the man on the research side of the organization. So a development background is not only a correlate of entrepreneurship but also a statement of experience applicable in an entrepreneurial undertaking.

Remember that these data are for companies formed typically about 1962. To the extent that readers believe 1973 is different from 1962 or 1963, they may argue that new phenomena and changed circumstances render our data obsolete. But we suspect that the obvious changes—the altered money market, the reduced availability of government contracts, new technologies not available ten years ago—are superficial, that most of our basic findings are as valid for companies formed today as for companies organized ten years ago.

The remainder of this book is devoted to providing experience-based guidelines to aspiring entrepreneurs. Some of this advice is even supportable from empirical research, but none of it is so unassailable as to preclude variations by venturesome entrepreneurs. Success in building a new enterprise can be reached via many different paths.

Edward B. Roberts*
Cambridge, Massachusetts
February 5, 1973

* Dr. Roberts received degrees in engineering, management, and economics from the Massachusetts Institute of Technology, culminating in a Ph.D. in economics in 1962. He presently holds the following positions: Professor of Management, M.I.T., Alfred P. Sloan School of Management, and chairman of its Technology and Health Management Group; president, Pugh-Roberts Associates, Inc. Professor Roberts is a director of several young technology-based enterprises and serves as a consultant to numerous industrial corporations in the fields of strategic planning, organization design, and the management of technical innovation. He has been a member of the Air Force Scientific Advisory Board, the Department of Commerce Technical Advisory Board, and a consultant to the President's Advisory Council on Management Improvement. Dr. Roberts is the author of numerous books and articles on various aspects of management.

ACKNOWLEDGMENTS

We have traced the origin and progress of several companies in this book, but we would be remiss if some of the history of the book itself were not presented as well. Like many good ideas, this one began with a need. In a dark and smoke-filled room one night, Fred Lehmann '51 and Panos Spiliakos '66 of the M.I.T. Alumni Office sat with another M.I.T. alumnus, Martin Schrage '63, trying to find some activity that would attract and serve young alumni. Martin Schrage was a member of the Class Activities Committee of the M.I.T. Alumni Association, which was chaired by Don Herter '46. After that night, the idea of a series of seminars on entrepreneurship evolved from conception to reality very much as a result of the efforts of these four men. As the idea gained momentum and spread to other cities, Fred Lehmann and Panos Spiliakos became the nerve centers for an immensely successful series of seminars on entrepreneurship that were held by alumni across the country. Nearly 1000 alumni participated in the hard work of presenting these seminars, and many more attended them.

When about three-quarters of the seminars had been given, I prepared an outline for a book based upon many of the exciting ideas presented at the seminars and my own experience as an entrepreneur. Then Fred Lehmann, and Panos Spiliakos, and I discussed with many other alumni the idea of

the Alumni Association publishing a book as a part of its
overall program. As a result of these discussions, we developed
a plan that included the selection of an editorial advisory
board composed of distinguished and successful entrepreneurs.
  The editorial board that we were able to bring together
included the following:

George M. Berman '45
President and Chairman of the Board
Unitrode Corporation

Kenneth J. Germeshausen '31
Consultant and Director
E.G.&G., Inc.

Donald R. Miller '50
Vice-President and Eastern Regional Manager
Cresap, McCormack and Paget

Richard S. Morse '33
Senior Lecturer
M.I.T. Sloan School of Management
President
M.I.T. Development Foundation, Inc.

Denis M. Robinson '31
Chairman, Board of Directors
High Voltage Engineering, Inc.

Arthur F. F. Snyder
President
Bank of the Commonwealth
Detroit, Michigan

Fred G. Lehmann '51
Director, M.I.T. Alumni Fund
Financial Vice-President
M.I.T. Alumni Association

Panos. D. Spiliakos '66
Entrepreneur, Greece
Formerly Assistant Secretary
M.I.T. Alumni Association

William D. Putt '59
President
Holograph Corporation
Editor of the Book

Each of the members of the editorial board reviewed the outline and the submitted chapters, contributing the time, effort, and thought necessary to produce a book of the quality we wished to attain. I would especially like to mention the assistance of Ken Germeshausen, who all through the process offered his ideas and encouragement. Finally, after contributing their chapters, the authors showed great patience throughout the many revisions and changes that were needed.

My own thanks and appreciation to all who contributed along the way cannot be adequately expressed in these few words. I hope, however, that the book will meet the expectations of all who participated in the entrepreneurship program and that it will reflect credit upon the Alumni Association.

William D. Putt

I THE BIRTH OF A NEW BUSINESS

This book grew in great measure from a series of seminars held by the M.I.T. Alumni Association for its alumni across the country. The intent was to draw the collective entrepreneurial experience of many alumni and friends of M.I.T. into an interesting and useful presentation for all those "would-be," current, and past entrepreneurs who chose to attend our seminars. We tried to attract as speakers not just successful entrepreneurs but also men who had experienced failure and just modest survival. We further sought the participation of many of those who service the new-venture field, such as attorneys, financiers, personnel recruiters, and others.

This was the most widely attended series of seminars ever presented by the M.I.T. Alumni Association. Somewhat to our surprise, the greatest number of those attending were people interested in starting their own businesses rather than men and women who had already founded their own firms.

In this book we have tried to capture the realism that developed in the seminars. Few of the authors are entrepreneurs of world renown, but all know their topics well, often from bitter experience. The book is aimed at the man or woman who is just beginning to think about starting his or her own business. It is not theoretical or blue-sky but rather an exciting collection of experience and practical knowledge.

Part I relates primarily to that period of time which occurs

before you start your own business. It is during this incuba-
tion period that commitment, ideas, and partners are tested.
Although a surprisingly large number of men and women
aspire to become entrepreneurs, only a small portion of them
actually cross the threshold. It is not easy to quit your job with
its steady income or to step out where failure as well as
success is yours alone. It is not easy to jeopardize your son's
education for your own ambition. It is not easy to undertake a
project for which you have had no real preparation or
experience. Make no mistake, being an entrepreneur is most
often a frustrating and unrewarding job. If you succeed, it
may not be worth the personal cost to you and your family. If
you fail, your whole promising career may be sacrificed.

Nevertheless, it is my feeling that very few potential
entrepreneurs pass up a real opportunity for any of the above
personal considerations. The first basic reason for this stems
from the fact that very little information is publicized about
the kinds of hardship that do result. Consequently, the
magnitude of the hardship tends to be underrated. Grief tends
to be more vivid in hindsight than in foresight. Second, the
mythology of entrepreneurship is that great personal sacrifice
will bring great wealth and fame. This, then, provides a
rationalization or justification for any anticipated sacrifice.

The most time-consuming part of the decision process for
most entrepreneurs is related to the business question of
whether a particular opportunity is the "true million-dollar
idea." Most people looking for such an idea do not evaluate it
in terms of detailed market, cost, and production analyses
because they have the feeling that the numbers can always be
made to look good. Rather, they try to decide whether the
idea can succeed on its own. Will people beat a path to my
door to buy this new product even if I do only a mediocre
management job? Do I have the next Polaroid camera or
Xerox machine?

The final hurdle for a prospective entrepreneur is choosing a partner or partners and then bringing in others on a straight employment basis. While this task is not one that holds potential entrepreneurs in the fantasy land of only wanting but never doing, it is one that should take time. When you are choosing partners, time is the best determinant of competence and compatibility.

Throughout this book you will encounter some widely divergent views on how best to begin your new venture. As an example, in the first part, Ray Stata emphasizes the importance of a single leader to avoid any confusion in the lines of authority. In contrast, Jim Stockwell and I emphasize the importance of supplementing the skills and abilities of the founder with those of other partners. We have not presented here a narrow channel to entrepreneurial success but rather an articulate collection of experiences that we believe will take much of the mystery out of starting a new company.

The aspiring entrepreneur may wonder if an "autobiographical" approach to start-up problems can help someone with a different product and a different set of circumstances. We think you will find, as we did, that start-up activities for many new businesses cover much of the same ground. All of us began with a strong desire to be on our own and to test our ideas and abilities in the open marketplace. Then, no matter what our product—a new marketing approach, a technological improvement for a product already on the market, or an original invention—most of us had to design market tests, choose business partners, find investors, resolve legal questions, develop our products, and plan our own promotion, marketing, and cost control programs. Certain considerations do not apply equally to every business, but the similarities among new ventures seem to outnumber the differences.

We think this book is unique because it is not a collection of success stories. Many of the authors are still only a few years beyond the start-up phase. They haven't yet had time to forget the problems of start-up or to romanticize them. It is this quality of immediacy that we hope to communicate to our readers. Although the book describes start-up activities in detail, they are not necessarily presented in the order in which you will want to tackle them. Each entrepreneur should be able to decide for himself how best to order the functional presentation once he understands its relationship to his company's needs. We have attempted throughout to provide insights that will save time, money, and risk.

William D. Putt

1 HOW DOES AN ENTREPRENEUR BEGIN?

Randall S. Robinson*

When I made up my mind to go into business on my own, the greatest problem was deciding how to begin. Although I don't usually agonize over decisions, my first year was a time of uncertainty and struggle. I felt that every mistake could have serious repercussions. Even though I had had an extensive technical and business education, military service, and five years of business experience, the problems of getting off the ground seemed tougher than most I had faced before.

How does a prospective entrepreneur go about launching a new enterprise? What, exactly, are the initial steps? It was precisely these rudimentary questions that were especially troublesome for me at the outset.

The same questions become important for virtually every new-business founder the first time around. So I shall offer some comments and suggestions about beginning from the beginning. In doing this, I shall draw upon my personal experiences and the experiences of others I know.

* Randall S. Robinson received his S.B. in general science from M.I.T. and his S.M. and Ph.D. degrees in management from M.I.T. He was the founder and is currently president of Robinson Information Technology Company. Dr. Robinson was chairman of the M.I.T. Alumni Association's national entrepreneur workshops in 1971.

The Decision to Become an Entrepreneur

The very first step, of course, is making the definite decision to take the plunge. Before you reach that decision, you should reflect on whether the entrepreneur's life is really for you and, if so, when is a suitable time to start.

The stereotype of a business founder is that of a great folk hero. Unless you have firsthand knowledge of working in a new enterprise, it is easy to conjure up a romanticized vision of what it's like.

Yes, you might make a lot of money. And the satisfaction you would derive from creating an enterprise from scratch could be tremendous. But, again, you might wind up without money and as the creator of a disaster. Furthermore, whether you succeed or fail, you probably will face trials and tribulations that surpass what you will encounter in a nonentrepreneurial career.

A successful entrepreneur must possess or develop certain personal qualities and strengths to meet the challenges he faces. For example, he must be willing and able to work nights and weekends. I remember a conversation I had with an entrepreneurially minded friend when we were both still employees. He said, "Boy, wouldn't it be great to be able to slip out for a round of golf any afternoon you felt in the mood?" I haven't played much golf since I started Robinson Information Technology. If you want more free time, you won't find it in a new venture—unless you aren't doing any business.

Another necessary strength is the capacity to handle anything and everything that comes up, including what some might view as menial or petty tasks. Unless your firm is one of the rare ones that is amply staffed, you probably will find yourself personnally immersed in the minutiae of daily activity, extending from licking stamps to cleaning floors.

More difficult is the ability to function well in the face of a high risk of failure. Most new businesses go through several periods of teetering on the brink of closing; many do close. For a while at least, the entrepreneur lives with a high degree of uncertainty about the fate of his business. He can expect to arrive at a number of occasions when his next day, or his next hour, looks like the last.

Closely related to the foregoing are the requisite qualities of confidence and persistence. Success stories you hear seldom highlight the setbacks experienced along the way. How many times was the entrepreneur's promising new product not fully developed because of insufficient funds? How many unsuccessful calls were made with an incomplete prototype? There are many rejections and disappointments involved in a new venture. You have to be able to bounce back after each one.

I think the quality of being open to feedback—from customers, investors, friends, and others—is crucially important. The founder's willingness to learn and change direction can be a vital factor in his success. For instance, it is not uncommon for a new business to radically revise its product or service line before it begins to click.

Although each of these personal strengths is vital, the fundamental question is not "Am I qualified to be an entrepreneur?" but rather "Am I willing to make sacrifices to be an entrepreneur?" Or, to put it another way, "Have I realistically assessed the costs and risks as well as the potential rewards?" Start-up probably will take longer than you expected; the expense is likely to be higher; the burden on your family probably will exceed your worst expectations. You may fail and have to walk away after three or four years of effort. These facts of life should be recognized before you make your decision.

Should your interest survive the rigorous screening just described, the next issue is that of choosing the right time. There is no time like the present! If you have a moderate amount of business experience, my advice is to begin preparation.

Other Steps in the Beginning

You have resolved to plan a new business. What next? The following list of suggested steps may help you chart your course at the very beginning:

1. *Set aside a period for preparation.* It is important to realize that preparation will require substantial time, even *before* your company becomes a legal entity—perhaps as long as six months to a year, or more. Be ready to invest the necessary hours and energy.

2. *Bring your family aboard.* It is best to have, from the beginning, the backing of your wife or husband and any other family members who will be directly affected. You will need their loyal support just when the problems of entrepreneurship are most disturbing to them—when you are preoccupied with the business to the exclusion of everything else, when you are spending long hours away from home, when your income is reduced, and when the future seems bleak. Although you cannot fully anticipate the wide range of problems that you may have to face together, you should at least try to be realistic.

3. *Work out the basic idea for your business.* Possibly you can develop a technological innovation in your present field or initiate a consulting practice with skills you have acquired during your career. Perhaps you will move out in a totally different direction. You may choose one idea and stick with it, or you may have to investigate and discard several ideas before you find one that is viable.

4. *Talk to your attorney.* He is the first person, outside your family, with whom to discuss your plans. Before making any oral or written agreements, and even before you let anyone

know that you are planning a new business venture, get your lawyer's advice. The attorney you consult for this purpose should be an expert in the legal problems of entrepreneurs. Keep him involved as you go along.

5. *Determine when and how you plan to depart from your job.* It is very important to maintain friendly relations with your present employer if at all possible. And if there is to be integrity in the way you do business, a good place to begin is by treating your employer as you will want to be treated when you become an employer.

6. *Line up the founders.* If your company is to try for fast growth, and particularly if you plan to solicit an investment from a source of venture capital, there ought to be two able founders right from the beginning, preferably more. At least one of you should be strong in marketing. Another point that comes up often, usually accompanied by a horror story, is that the founders at the outset should agree on who is going to be head of the company and, furthermore, on how the responsibilities will be allocated. Stay away from the we-are-all-equal, everybody-does-everything approach.

7. *Talk to your banker.* He should be one who does business with start-up companies. Your banker can be a valuable source of referrals, advice, and in some instances even loans at the earliest stages.

8. *Make arrangements for proper accounting.* You can live with primitive records and minimal accounting knowledge during the early days of preparation. But when you assemble a business plan for the scrutiny of enlightened equity investors, and when you begin doing business with a view toward growth culminating, say, in an offering of stock to the public, you need accounting expertise.

9. *Prepare a comprehensive plan for your company's development.* This should include your marketing strategy, estimates of financial requirements, and projections of growth in sales. In order to

put this plan together, you must think through the major details of how your business will operate, with emphasis on marketing. You probably won't be able to afford a market study in the depth to which a big company is accustomed, but you should, nevertheless, talk with some potential customers and otherwise do as much as you can to evaluate the distribution and selling of your product or service.

10. *Raise the funds necessary to start your company.* There is no better feasibility test for a new business, short of selling your product to a customer, than to convince an investor to place his money in your project. You will begin with your own money and money from other founders, of course; that may be—or have to be—sufficient throughout your preparation and even throughout early operations. Should you solicit backing from professional investors, you will require a thorough proposal, or business plan. Check on potential investors; to the degree that you can be selective, you should choose those who are going to be helpful and stay with you during hard times.

Success as an entrepreneur comes from an indefinable blend of skill, hard work, timing, persistence, dedication, and daring. Also luck. The prospective business founder cannot eliminate the impact of luck, but he can diminish its effect. The completion of sound, thoughtful preparation is an important means of doing this.

2 OPENING STRATEGIES

Raymond S. Stata*

There are several schools of thought about starting your own business. At one end of the spectrum are those people who will advise you to analyze every aspect of your future business down to the smallest detail and to wait until you are 90 percent certain of success before stepping out on your own. On the other side are those who say: strike quickly, regardless of the odds, when you know intuitively that you have found a good situation. To give a little more operational meaning to these divergent approaches, I will describe three alternative start-up plans, each of which I have pursued in my own career as an entrepreneur.

Plan A: The Experiment

If you are confident of your ability to get another job and are still fairly young and willing to risk failure, what can you lose? If you believe in your ideas, plunge in and see what happens. I believe that a very talented entrepreneur will succeed almost regardless of where he starts. The point is just to start. Expose yourself to the opportunities and challenges that spring up. A person who is not cut out for this kind of life will soon know it,

* Ray Stata received his S.B. and S.M. in electrical engineering from M.I.T. He was a cofounder of Solid State Instruments, Inc., and later a cofounder of Analog Devices, Inc., whose sales now exceed $30 million.

even if he has all of the aces on Day One. For Plan A, you should not waste a lot of time looking for the best of all possible worlds with regard to partners and the terms of your financing. Bargain for the best terms you can get, and then do something. This may sound reckless, but it worked for me, and I've seen it work for others.

Plan B: The Two-Step

This is Plan A with a slight twist. The entrepreneur starts his company with the intention of selling it and starting over again on the proceeds. There are several factors that might convince you to select this strategy. Perhaps you do not have enough capital to go it alone, or the terms for raising capital are unattractive. Possibly you need more experience, and the chances for the type of accelerated on-the-job training that you need are nil in your present position, unless three people suddenly die. Or perhaps you are not positive that the new venture is exactly right for you, and you want to retain a few ties to the harbor before cutting out for the open sea. For this plan, a joint venture with a going company is one of the better approaches. You may be surprised how reasonable a deal you can negotiate if you have something to offer. Usually, the company invests cash with an option to buy the remainder of your stock at some later time. If you perform well, you may end up with a nice nest egg to use in starting over again. Since later on you will want liquidity, be careful to select a company with negotiable stock.

Another approach is to obtain your initial funding from noncorporate venture capital sources. To limit your risk in the first company, you are better off seeking as much money as possible at the sacrifice in equity. In this type of situation, taking on more, rather than fewer, partners is advisable, since you are looking for as much help as possible to achieve an early success.

Plan C: Preparing for the Long Haul

In spite of my advocacy of Plans A and B, they are compromises at best, acceptable alternatives if there is no other way to begin. Obviously, where life will allow the luxury, the best idea is to keep searching until you find the "right" situation: a good product, capital, and a well-organized marketing strategy. The problem is that every opportunity is relative, and it is difficult to be sure that further searching will not turn up an even better alternative. Nevertheless, Plan C is for the entrepreneur who is willing to wait for the opportunity to build a sound, long-term business.

If you are planning for the long haul, measure your decisions by this basic rule: Do not compromise your flexibility. This means you should not take on *any* partners or give out any stock options. You should raise the absolute minimum of money from outside sources in order to hold on to as much equity as possible. This may mean a riskier start-up, but it will also mean that you are in control of your own company.

In the earliest stages of start-up, the value of your company's stock will be negligible. But value increases rapidly with even the most meager accomplishment. If you quit your present job, spend $300 to incorporate, rent a building, and hang out a shingle, you are creating value. You are also making it clear to potential associates that *you* are in charge. If you can finance the development of your product with your own money, you are making a healthy start. If you can book even one purchase order, you are on your way to convincing investors that you have a viable operation. Go as far as you can before looking for outside backing. And then fight to hold on to a major share of ownership, even if it means less working capital.

The opposition to this line of reasoning is usually something like this: Most companies fail because they are undercapitalized. Therefore, the entrepreneur should try to raise a little extra money in the beginning as insurance against failure. I categorically reject this advice. You never get something for nothing. You will pay dearly for that "extra" money. For Plan C, in order to strengthen your bargaining position, your job is to stretch your seed money as far as possible before looking for more. Don't make any decisions that will limit your maneuverability.

A First Attempt

My first experience as an entrepreneur started out as a Plan A strategy but quickly evolved into a Plan B. With no viable product or market plan, almost no capital ($3000), and very little experience, two partners and I (average age: twenty-eight) launched our business. But we did have enthusiasm, energy, and an irresistible drive to be on our own. We were looking for any excuse to quit our jobs and begin our own enterprise. The excuse, when it came, was very feeble indeed— some short-term opportunities growing out of the work we were already doing. During our first year we survived on pure grit. By most measures our enterprise was a fiasco. Nevertheless, within a year we found a company willing to acquire our business in exchange for $120,000 of their stock. We were made vice-presidents of our company and given two-year employment contracts as well as good salaries.

The corporation that acquired us was less interested in our company than in our sales and engineering experience. We had tapped a market that they had also identified as a growth market. We had the requisite skill, after a year, to develop it. What's more, they were impressed by our irrepressible enthusiasm and our ability to create something out of nothing. We produced a reasonable return on their investment in two years and, at the same time, learned a great deal about starting and operating a small company. When our contract expired, two of us left to pursue Plan C. We formed Analog Devices with the capital acquired from the merger, and over the next eight years we produced more than $20,000,000 in sales.

Examining Motives and Goals

In retrospect, many a successful entrepreneur would find it hard to justify his initial decision to start his own company— that is, if business issues were his sole concern. On the basis of my own experience, I am convinced that they are not.

Several motives are usually ascribed to the entrepreneur—the quest for independence, wealth, status, fame, and the urge to create and develop a unique concept. But all of these goals can be satisfied by other means. After all, the president of General Electric is virtually his own boss—and is rich and famous, too. So, to varying degrees, are many professional managers. The key to the entrepreneur's drive is his need for *autonomy*. He seeks freedom to work out his own plans and will take incredible risks to achieve his own goals. When he is in control, he thrives on challenge. He is at his best when the odds are against him. He also immerses himself almost totally in his business and does not distinguish between personal success and his company's success. For him, the company is not an entity "out there." It is an extension of himself.

A professional manager often feels much more detached about his company. His outside life may be as important to him as his job, perhaps more so. He does not judge his personal success solely in terms of his company's success. But the entrepreneur does not achieve, or seek, this distance. He makes an extraordinary emotional commitment to his company, which is more important than his (also extraordinary) commitment of money and time. When circumstances force a choice between family and firm, it is surprising how often the firm wins.

How does the entrepreneur measure success? If financial

independence were his only goal, the answer would be obvious. But many an entrepreneur whose company has achieved outstanding success remains slavishly devoted to his business. Others who successfully sell their companies return to the game again when their employment contracts have expired.

Shortly after my partners and I had sold our first company and were working for someone else, I began to question the purpose of my work. For the first time, the company's goals and my personal goals were in conflict. Before the merger, I had confronted problems that seemed insurmountable. I was constantly frustrated and exasperated. Yet there was enormous satisfaction in knowing that I could shape the company's goals and direct its activity. After the merger, a one-to-one relationship no longer existed. As soon as I could, I left the company and formed a new one.

Relationships with Partners

The entrepreneur's need for autonomy makes conflict with business partners inevitable. In many cases, however, the entrepreneur needs partners if there is to be any company at all. Since start-up and survival problems are so demanding, personal difficulties can be ignored at first. But once the company is on course, each partner becomes more attentive to his own needs. If each is motivated by the same need for autonomy, someone is going to be disappointed. There will eventually be some kind of blowup unless this problem is anticipated before the company is formed. Conflicts among partners may destroy an otherwise healthy venture. Or, even worse, unresolved conflicts may go underground, surfacing at times of stress, causing personal unhappiness and interfering with company goals. In the long run, partnerships are bad news.

If you must have partners, make sure from the very beginning that inequality exists and is recognized—if not in ownership of stock, then in the designation of leadership and authority. One partner is about the limit. With two or more, you're in for real trouble.

In my first company, all the partners were equal, and the president was picked by flipping a coin. We made the naïve assumption that this office would rotate annually, a very convenient way to avoid the question of leadership. Communication between two partners is difficult, but agreement can usually be reached through a process of give-and-take. Among three people communication is impossible. You seldom can reach a unanimous agreement. Someone almost always ends up on the losing side of a two-to-one vote. The result is an environment fraught with insecurity. A coffee break shared by two partners is interpreted by the third as the start of a conspiracy. If unanimity among partners is established as a hard-and-fast rule, decisions may never be made. This is disastrous: any decision is usually better than none at all. And if you think the partners are having a difficult time, try to imagine how an employee feels in this environment. Everyone in the company is affected by conflict at the top.

In my second company, partnership conflicts became less intense because there were only two of us. Nevertheless, the basic problem was not resolved. Our first experience should have taught us something, but once again we ignored the need to choose one boss. This time, we divided the company in half, each partner having total authority in his own fiefdom. This actually worked pretty well in the early days. Decisions on company-wide issues were made after a give-and-take exchange. But within our separate areas of responsibility, decisions were made unilaterally, without sufficient coordination. As the company grew, this separation caused severe problems. Privately, we referred to our business as the two-headed monster. But though we knew the situation was bad for the company, neither of us could accept the other as "the boss." Eventually, we admitted that the company would be better off if one of us left, and my partner did.

To give credit where it is due, some partnerships have endured and prospered: witness Hewlett-Packard and Tektronics. Many firms—other than professional partnerships— have three or more names in the company title. But I am convinced that in these companies the relationship between the partners was thoroughly defined from the beginning, with one partner clearly the leader.

To some extent, everyone has a spark of entrepreneurship. Modern management practice recognizes this spirit and strives to establish an environment where professional managers are left to do their own thing to the greatest possible extent. Companies are doing a better job of satisfying the entrepreneurial needs of their employees, and most people are able to pursue their careers within this framework. Before you break out on your own, be sure you recognize that everything has its price—and in this case the price is a hellish devotion and commitment if you are going to be successful. Your family and other interests are bound to suffer, at least to some extent. Think about this in depth before choosing your own variation of Plan A, B, or C.

3 TESTING THE MARKET AND CHOOSING BUSINESS PARTNERS

William D. Putt*

The scientific genius who invents an extraordinary new product while toiling in the obscurity of a giant corporation's R&D laboratory has become a staple of twentieth-century business mythology. Throwing off the shackles of his bureaucratic employer, he strikes out on his own, struggles to find financial and managerial assistance, starts a dynamic new enterprise, earns several million dollars, and is toasted by *Fortune* and *Business Week* as the "entrepreneur of the year."

A different version of the story does not make front-page news but may be closer to the truth: the entrepreneur chooses a partner, whom he gradually grows to distrust, he can't find a market for his product; his original employer sues him for stealing company secrets; he loses his lifetime savings; and his wife files for divorce.

Before he arrives at either point, and before his business can get off the ground, the aspiring entrepreneur must tackle and resolve several fundamental problems. He must select a product or service idea for his company. He must test it and convince himself and others of its market potential. Finally, he must choose one or more business partners.

* William D. Putt received his S.B., S.M., and Ph.D. degrees in management from M.I.T. In 1968 he was a founder of Holograph Corporation. He is currently president of Holograph Corporation.

The Million-Dollar Idea

In my own experience, I have seen ideas for new companies generated in three different ways. The aspiring entrepreneur may start by selecting several markets that have high growth potential. After selecting these markets, he will then analyze their entry requirements and his own strengths and weaknesses vis-à-vis these markets. Ultimately, one market segment is selected, and the genesis of the business is under way.

I know two entrepreneurs who chose this strategy while still in college. They studied many industrial statistics and decided to focus on the computer time-sharing market, copiers, video cassette systems, and several other growing industries. After further research, they singled out the equipment segment of the computer time-sharing market. A plan was developed to manufacture and distribute a portable CRT computer terminal, to be priced lower than any other on the market. Neither of the aspiring entrepreneurs had experience in the design or manufacture of computer hardware, but both were strong in marketing and finance. They attracted people with excellent technical skills to their venture and together were able to raise sufficient capital to launch their business. This was clearly a case in which industrial growth potential was considered more important than personal experience.

A second, more common, approach reverses the order of consideration and importance. The entrepreneur assesses his own strengths before turning his attention to market factors. A set of markets is chosen that complements the entrepreneur's capabilities without regard to growth rates. Only after these markets have been selected does the entrepreneur rank them for growth, if there is more than one.

Following this second approach, a research associate in a large university that I attended decided that he would like to capitalize on his extensive education and research activities. His entire professional life, though still relatively short, had been spent in analyzing sophisticated financial management problems. He discussed his plans with potential customers, many of whom he had met while engaged in his own research, and eventually formed his own consulting firm.

A third approach is based on the discovery or invention of a unique product or idea. My own company, Holograph Corporation, grew out of such a strategy. My partner, Harry Forster, began to develop the original idea in 1965. At that time he was an independent consultant, working for the State of New Jersey on traffic problems related to the New Jersey Turnpike. One evening, during a bull session with several engineers working for the state, the problem of making signs on the turnpike visible under fog conditions was brought up. At various times in the past, plans to sweep away fog and to reflect signs off the fog had been considered, but these ideas ranged from infeasible to impossible. On this particular evening, Harry suggested that holograms might be used to project signs into the road. Images of signs would be projected at a distance that would give motorists sufficient time to avoid driving into the posts and standards holding the signs.

No one in the group had studied the technical feasibility of holographic signs. Harry, a highly capable engineer and theoretician, had been reading in the area of holography and was excited by the possibilities.

Testing the Market

Once an idea is born, the entrepreneur must find out if there is a market for it. One way to do this is to discuss the product with potential customers. If they are very interested, they may write a "letter of intent to purchase." If they are moderately interested, they may be persuaded to write a "letter of interest." Any sort of letter from a potential customer will help the entrepreneur when he is looking for financial backing.

Talking with distributors can also be helpful. They hear a

wide variety of complaints and requests and may know what product innovations would appeal to customers.

It is sometimes informative to advertise for manufacturers' representatives for your product. A reasonable number of responses from established representatives may be an indication that your product will sell. If there seems to be a lack of interest, however, find out if your product lacks credibility or if representatives are simply unwilling to work for a fledgling enterprise, one that may not be in business long enough to deliver their orders.

You may decide to write an article about your product or an advertisement. It is interesting to find out if you can predict the types of people who will respond and the kinds of questions they will ask. Although they may inquire about features of your product that seem elementary to you, their questions will tell you what customers want to know before making a purchase.

You should attend professional meetings. They are often dull—unless you are one of the speakers—but you may find people who are willing to listen and to help.

An especially important market test involves some interaction with the competition. Read your competitors' brochures. Study trends in the industry. Present yourself as a potential customer, and find out what improvements your competitors are planning for their products. Visit trade shows. At most of them, companies will give you the keys to the store. Or try to sell your own idea to a competitor. Companies are frequently interested in buying new ideas. The exposure will let you know how your product looks to someone already in the field.

The market for holographic signs was tested in several ways, although my partner first thought of his idea as the basis for a consulting contract rather than a new business. Encouraged by discussions with New Jersey highway officials, he applied to the U.S. Department of Transportation for a contract to explore

the concept. A small contract was awarded to Forster Industries, the forerunner of the Holograph Corporation, and the
study was completed in the latter part of 1967. The Department of Transportation library customarily sends news releases
to all highway publications when a new study is filed. Shortly
after its completion, Harry's report was summarized in a
one-paragraph article in a small highway periodical under the
title "Signs Without Posts." The response was instantaneous.
Inquiries came from state highway departments, from universi-
ties, and from industry. Unexpectedly, Harry had the beginning of a real market test for his idea.

Although the report was a public document, Harry preferred
not to distribute it widely since it included some original
technical information. He thought it would be useful, however,
to test the concept on a larger population, and submitted an
article to a well-known trade journal. In the article, he gave his
product a name: Holosign. The timing was fortuitous. A short
time before, Congress had criticized the highway profession for
its lack of technological innovation. As a result, the editors of
the journal were receptive to an article describing a technology
new to the highway field. Harry's article was published in
1968. It generated both enthusiasm and skepticism. People
unfamiliar with the field of holography were tremendously
excited. They wrote to ask whether he had already built any
signs, where they could see them, when they could buy them,
and how much they would cost. Individuals knowledgeable in
the field of holography were more reserved in their response.
Nevertheless, the number of letters generated by the article
convinced him that he had something more than an idea for a
consulting contract.

I had been working informally with Harry on the concept of
holographic signs since 1965. At the same time, I held a
position with a large consulting firm in Massachusetts and was
studying for a graduate degree in management. Although

Harry and I had often talked of starting a business together, only after the publication of his article did we think that holographic signs might give us the opportunity. We decided then to test the market more systematically. First, we determined the number of traffic signs produced annually in the United States. Then we found out how much money was allotted each year for traffic signs as part of the national highway construction program. We investigated the possibility of bidding for a federal research and development contract. We also visited highway agencies in several states. Since Harry was a recognized authority in the highway field and a member of the national Highway Research Board, highway officials were receptive to his ideas and encouraged us to develop them further. All this activity confirmed our belief that we had a product with enormous potential. There remained one crucial test: Could we build one?

Using our own money and working at odd hours, we rented an old delicatessen, converted the basement into a laboratory, and built a cement stable table with Styrofoam cushion absorbers and heavy aluminum mounts. We bought a laser and some high-resolution film and tried to make hologram highway signs. By the beginning of 1969, both of us were working full time on the project. Although we discovered that we could not use holographic techniques to produce our signs, other fields of optics yielded the techniques we needed to simulate certain of the desired holographic effects. After several months, we were able to build a prototype. The effort cost the two of us $25,000 and a considerably larger amount of lost salary. But after two years, we were ready to form a company.

Choosing Business Partners

No matter how dynamic his product, the entrepreneur usually finds it hard to raise money on his own. A potential investor is often more willing to invest his money with a partnership. One reason is that he wants to know if the entrepreneur can work effectively with other people to develop and market his product. When two or more partners approach him together, he assumes that they have developed a comfortable working relationship.

You may ask whether, if two partners are a good idea, twenty partners would be ten times better. Not long ago, a friend of mine formed a company with fourteen other equal partners. After a year, two of the fifteen realized that their leadership abilities were responsible for the growth of the business. They asked themselves why they were breaking their backs and taking salary cuts when they owned only 5 percent of company stock. Eventually, one of them left to form his own business. The original company then experienced a difficult period of adjustment. In other words, if your partners do not feel they are being adequately compensated for their efforts, they will probably leave the company. Once they have learned how to start a new business, they can easily strike out on their own if they are dissatisfied. This is important to remember when you are deciding how many partners the company can support.

There are four questions to ask yourself when you are evaluating a prospective partner: What are his capabilities? Are the two (or more) of you compatible? Is he committed to the business? What kind of compensation will he require? You can't read a résumé or talk to a man for an hour or two to determine his worth. Before a commitment of ownership or partnership is made, work with him for a few months or even a year if possible. Give him specific technical or management tasks. Ask him to write a section of the financial proposal and to set up meetings with potential investors and customers. Above all, take time. His investment will, in part, be the time he gives you in this pre-start-up period.

How do you test compatibility? Many people will advise you

to avoid friends and relatives when looking for partners, since sentiment may cloud your ability to evaluate their capabilities. My opinion is that old friends are the first resource to explore because you already know they are compatible. No matter who the prospective partner is, assess his strengths in terms of your own. If he is aggressive and you are reserved, will this help or hurt the partnership? Does at least one of you like to talk to people—investors, customers, distributors, suppliers—or would you both prefer to bury yourselves in the lab? (*Somebody* has to get out there and hustle your product.) Since you will be working through some tough problems together, it is important to know how a potential partner reacts to stress. Try criticizing his work, setting some deadlines, asking for small amounts of money when they are needed.

It is not easy to judge another person's commitment. New companies are exciting: perhaps yours looks like the one that will make a million dollars. Lots of people will be willing to go along for the ride if it doesn't cost anything or take any time. Or they may be willing to work for a new company if the salary is higher than their present salary. But this tells you nothing about their commitment to the new venture.

Is your prospective partner willing to contribute his time before any money is coming in? Will he write proposals, prepare sales forecasts, conduct technical studies, put up the walls of the new office, or shovel the driveway when it snows? Will he make cold sales calls? Is he willing to put his reputation on the line, to be known as part of the company? Will he put up $500 or $1000 even before you have negotiated specific partnership terms? Will he take a day or two off from his job to work on company projects—not a vacation day or a day that suits his schedule, but a day when you really need his help? Will he make some out-of-town trips and spend a night or two away from home? I think he should be willing to do all of these things even before the specific terms of your relationship are spelled out, if he is committed to the enterprise.

Find out the circumstances under which he will leave his present job. Will he quit the new company at the first sign of difficulty?

Finally, you will have to decide when to discuss compensation. I recommend that you wait as long as possible. Evaluate your prospective partner's abilities, compatibility, and commitment first. The closer you are to the establishment of your company, the better your negotiating position. A potential partner must decide how much your idea is worth before determining how much he needs for his share. If you have a $50,000 idea, he may need 50 percent. If your product is worth a million dollars a year, 10 percent may satisfy him.

When you are negotiating financial terms, make several proposals. Try to set up a bargaining situation in which no one will feel he is the "winner" or the "loser." But decide ahead of time what your own limits will be—the lowest and highest amount you are willing to offer or accept.

In addition to these rather subjective aspects of appraising a prospective partner, it is always a good idea to check his Dun and Bradstreet rating and to talk with his employers and his bank. Several years ago, I participated in the acquisition of a company with someone whom I had known only too briefly. He had received high recommendations from trusted sources, however. After a disastrous experience, I learned that he had entered the negotiations hoping for a quick withdrawal of cash to satisfy pressing personal debts. Furthermore, he had been accused of illegal business transactions some years earlier. The company survived, but it was a hard way to learn the necessity for investigating a potential partner's background thoroughly.

Harry Forster's approach to selecting partners for the Holograph Corporation was typical, I believe. When the potential of "holographic" signs became apparent, he invited six friends and associates to help him develop a company around his idea. The group included men with strong technical, marketing, and financial abilities. I had been a friend of Harry's since our

undergraduate days and was one one of the people he
approached. We were all invited to participate in the start-up
process on weekends and, later, for longer periods. Harry asked
us to help in writing proposals, developing the product, raising
money, making sales, and defining the business. He found that
some assignments were done well; others, not so well. The
problem was that several people were inconsistent. When they
had free time, they were happy to work on the project. But
family, job, and recreational activities always took precedence.
This is a good way to tell if a prospective partner is willing to
make sacrifices for the new enterprise. But it would be a
mistake to reject anyone too early. It takes a certain length of
time for a person to become so committed to a venture that he
is willing to change his life-style.

Further along in the development of the business, Harry
needed small amounts of money to pay rent, hire a secretary,
send out mailings, and so forth. He periodically asked us to
help—not with large sums, but as much as $100 or $200 at a
time. He also asked us to take some time off from our jobs to
visit potential investors and customers.

After several months, Harry decided to formalize the company's structure. We all worked together on the terms of
incorporation and the division and price of company stock.
Harry had the final say on all decisions. We determined that
any partner who decided to withdraw from the company must
sell his stock back to the company at its original price. Harry
then offered ownership to several people. All of us were
interested, but some balked at the investment of $700 to $1000
for stock before more conclusive product tests were made.
When the negotiations came to an end, Harry and I were the
only ones left. Harry then proposed terms that I found
reasonable. The split was approximately 65 percent for him
and 35 percent for me.

It might well be asked why I did not request 49, 50, or 51

percent, since there were only two of us remaining as founders of the company. Several considerations influenced my thinking about the appropriate percentage. The first was that, as the creator of the idea around which the company was being built, Harry was contributing more to the formation of the company than I was. Second, I was not concerned about management control at that stage of the company's history, since I felt that on important issues I would be able to exert a certain amount of reason to affect such decisions. Third, I believed that if a voting confrontation developed, I could form a coalition with the investors of outside funding, which was going to be required. Finally, although Harry originally offered me 40 to 45 percent of the company, I turned it down because I thought doing so would solidify our working relationship. I also felt that 35 percent was sufficient to allow me to earn a great sum of money if we achieved our goals.

Since such percentage decisions are based on each person's aspirations and the merits of the situation, it will be very useful to compare some of the diverse philosophies presented in other chapters of this book. Ray Stata's approach in Chapter 2 is in direct contrast to the direction that I took here.

4 GROWTH THROUGH TECHNICAL DEVELOPMENT
Russell L. Haden, Jr.*

In a new venture, product development is often carried on before the company actually becomes a formal entity, and it continues during most of the start-up period. The entrepreneur should recognize that the initial goal of product development is not a "perfect" product. Rather, it is important to get a product on the market as soon as possible. As long as it works satisfactorily, you will be able to judge its market acceptability *before* you spend time in perfecting it. You may find that customers reject certain features entirely and want improvements in others. Further development will be guided by feedback from the field, saving you time and money.

Information from customers may also help you to develop companion products that enhance the basic product and to promote sales. For example, when I was involved in the early marketing of an instrument to measure water pollution, a customer suggested an add-on option that greatly increased the instrument's utility. In the instrument, a water sample was vaporized, burned in an oven with an excess of oxygen, and then absorbed, with the results measured chemically. The customer pointed out the virtues of making an infrared analysis of the vapor before absorption. We had thought of the burning

* Russell L. Haden, Jr., received his S.B. and S.M. in chemical engineering from M.I.T. He was president of Ionics, Inc., and is currently president of the Perolin Co., Inc.

process only as a step necessary for chemical analysis, not as a way of conducting a further useful analysis. (Oliver Wendell Holmes had a bit of relevant advice: Never overlook the obvious in the search for the obscure.)

Companion products give you something new to sell. You will appreciate this when your sales curve drops after your product has had its first rush of market acceptance. In any field, there are always a few customers who will buy something new. Some just like to be first. Others have such huge problems that they will try anything. These "pioneers" will give your sales curve its first boost. As they test your product, they can provide you with data that will help you to promote sales to the tougher, more critical customers who form the bulk of your market. All this takes time, and companion products can fill the gap between the first and subsequent versions of your product.

Funding Research and Development

Once you move from research to development, you have some basic decisions to make. Be assured that development will cost a lot of money—inevitably more than your most extravagant guess. Plan for that overrun, and examine your funding options. Here are some possibilities:
1. Raise your money through equity or debt financing, using the prototype developed during your research stage to obtain favorable terms.
2. Using the research prototype, seek out a production contract against which development costs can be amortized. Borrow against the contract to get early funds.
3. Apply for an R&D contract from a government agency.
4. Set up a joint venture with a larger company.

Naturally, there is risk involved in equity or debt financing. If your development is not completed with the money available, future investors or lenders will drive an even harder bargain.

But if you have other products in your line, you can always pause and wait for internal cash flow to provide funds for continued development. A production contract is even riskier because any mistakes made during development are multiplied as production begins.

There are several drawbacks to a government contract. You may have to give up almost all commercial rights. Your rate of reimbursement will be slow. And you will have to compromise your technical development to accommodate the views of the government supervisor. Nevertheless, this may be an acceptable route if the insights you gain can be put to commercial advantage.

When Ionics, Inc.'s primary business was desalting, we found it hard to accept the limits placed on us in projects sponsored by the Office of Saline Water (OSW), an agency in the Department of Health, Education, and Welfare. OSW's mandate was to promote new processes and new competition in the field of desalting. We decided to seek OSW contracts—after much soul-searching—because basic research was needed and because money was not available from other sources. In the course of intense negotiations for two 18-month contracts, we were able to narrow the definition of "subject field"—that is, the area to which restrictions on commercial development would be applied. We were also able to gain foreign patent rights. It is always important in such negotiations to insist on knowing *why* restrictions on commercial development are being imposed, even if you have to study the wording of the enabling legislation. If your engineering development is relatively complete and you have good background patents, a government contract can help you build a pilot plant for a field test. The contract should not be dangerous commercially if concessions involve only foreground (future) patent rights and test data.

In considering a joint venture with another firm, there are

two basic matters to evaluate. First, the established firm should be able to provide not only money but other strengths that you lack—perhaps entry into a particular market. For example, to develop a process for air pollution control, Ionics, Inc., entered into an agreement with a large architect/engineering firm. Since the primary market for the process would be electric utilities, which are traditionally conservative in accepting new concepts, our link with a large, reputable firm gave us credibility. We benefited from its reputation for thoroughness, as well as the engineering checks the company provided on our development work. The second consideration in forming a joint venture is whether you will be able to get out of it if the other company does not live up to its side of the bargain. If your partner is a large company and if the joint project is only a small part of its total business, it just may not push diligently ahead. You should negotiate terms that enable you to dissolve the partnership without losing control of your product should the venture prove unsatisfactory.

Marketing Feedback

As development progresses, it is critical to "close the loop"—to cross-check your assumptions constantly with the people who will be your customers. Dewey & Almy developed a new type of "blanket" for use in offset printing. Instead of distorting to receive an image as the standard, all-rubber blanket did, the new product compressed and thus transferred a clearer impression of the image. The Lithographic Technical Foundation (LTF), a research organization supported by the offset industry, was extremely enthusiastic about the improvement. Dewey & Almy's development was guided by LTF's tests, and the product was taken in finished form to the marketplace. Only then did we learn about the product's flaws in sustained use. Too late, we realized that we should have given some of our blankets to commercial printers *during* the development phase. Each journeyman printer has firmly entrenched habits. He retains a great deal of individual control over his press and may spend a lot of time improving the quality of a printed page if he doesn't like the way it looks. His supervisor cannot stay with him all the time, and so the printer himself controls the actual process. Our two-piece blanket made better quality possible, but it involved new techniques. Thus the printer had to develop new skills, and many of them resisted the change. Before our product was accepted, we had to go back to the lab and produce a one-piece (but still compressible) blanket more like the product the printer was used to. In their enthusiasm about our product's technical advantages, LTF's technical people had ignored the psychology of the pressmen who would be using the product. Early testing under normal conditions would have saved us time and money.

Chemical engineers use a technique of successive approximations in dealing with unknowns. This process is also useful in new product development. Here are some guidelines. First, develop a concept and price it out, making comparisons with a similar process, product, technique, and so forth. Second, if you have the time and money, make a market survey to test the acceptability of the concept and the projected price. Third, make a breadboard prototype and check pricing again. Fourth, rebuild your prototype according to your revised price schedule; then make another market survey.

What if you have neither the time nor the money to make a full-scale market survey once you have built a prototype? In this case, you might choose two prospective customers for a "minisurvey." Select one who is adventurous, ahead of the market, willing to try new things. Select another who is likely to be critical and conservative. Sit down with each separately and go over every aspect of your prototype, point by point. When you have rebuilt your prototype to incorporate their suggestions, check it out again with the same two prospects.

By using successive approximations, by listening hard, and by being flexible enough to accommodate criticism, you should be able to develop a product that will sell.

These are some of the factors you will have to identify during product development:

1. What basic customer need are you trying to satisfy?

2. Which of your product's features are basic requirements for satisfying that need?

3. Which additional features can be offered as options for an additional price? Which can be offered in the "second-generation" model? If an option is offered, what is its estimated value?

4. What support services must be offered to make the product useful to customers? (Perhaps your instrument needs a calibration service. Perhaps you can make punched cards to go with a computer, or toner to go with a copier.) The customer must have a complete operational system.

5. What is the *next best* thing a customer can buy to fill the need you have identified? (This is a version of the quality control concept of "marginal pass versus marginal reject.") By identifying a customer's alternatives, you can measure the value of your own product.

6. If the next-best alternative is a competing product, find out everything you can about its performance features and its price schedule, including less obvious pricing mechanisms such as special volume prices and sales promotion incentives. Perhaps your chief competitor offers support services, such as field engineering, or product improvement through R&D. Remember that every pioneering product needs a great deal of support—to convince skeptics and to defuse critics. Marketing experts at Procter & Gamble claim that it takes at least ten satisfied customers actively talking up a product to offset each customer who knocks it.

7. How much will it cost to build the product? To add or subtract features? To improve component quality? To reduce maintenance?

In developing a desalting unit to be used for a home water supply, Ionics was able to answer questions 1 through 4 above without any trouble. Our product was much smaller than the industrial units on the market at the time. But question 5—What is the next-best thing a customer can buy?—pulled us up short. During market tests in California, we discovered that our customers' needs could be satisfied by using a bottled water delivery service for potable water and a water softener for laundry and bath water. This meant that there was a ceiling on what the customer would pay for our desalting unit. This dollar ceiling was just too low for us, and we had to reduce the scope of our project drastically.

Another project was a small electrolytic chlorine generator for swimming pools. We started with the premise that the customer's basic need was a completely automatic method for keeping his pool chemically clean (questions 1 and 2). We knew that the "next-best" product was a low-priced automatic dry feeder of hypochlorite (questions 5 and 6). It would clean the pool, but not well. Our test marketing was aimed as discovering what other needs our product could satisfy. There were two. Our product cost less to operate, because hypochlorite is expensive. Our unit also gave the pool water a better "feel." However, to offset the low purchase price of the competing unit, we had to develop our product so that its purchase price could be reduced without increasing the customer's maintenance costs, since operating savings were to be the unit's most outstanding feature.

The final refining (question 7 above) often involves substantial expense. Breadboard working models are usually spread out and fully instrumented. The market model always has more difficulties. To reduce the price, the unit has to be squeezed into a small volume, with parts left out and many substitutions made. No matter how many months, or years, have been spent in testing the prototype, the market model will be affected by a "better idea" at the last minute, or by customer demands.

At some point during the course of product development, you must make—and *sell*—a limited production run. Whether this will be two or 200 will depend on the type of product you are developing. Customers who are testing free models just don't complain the way paying customers do. You'll learn a lot more if you charge. If a customer won't pay your asking price, reduce it—as an "introductory offer," or for the privilege of frequent inspections. Use any rationale that will convince the customer to buy. In the process of selling this limited production run, you will have to devise a distribution system pricing strategy. Remember that the cost of the distribution system figures prominently in the final cost of the product. For the electrolytic swimming pool chlorine generator described above, costs are still being worked out. We had originally expected to make direct sales, but we are now thinking of renting the unit for three months, allowing the customer to make full payment or to return the unit at the end of the three months. This will give him time to appreciate the operating savings and the improved quality of the water.

Scheduling Development

The phase of product development that involves market surveys and a limited production run costs far more than your initial research stage. And the time it takes will be longer than you expect. It will not take a major crisis to delay you—such as waiting for a Rolls Royce engine for your Lockheed 1011. It takes only little things to trip you up—a truck strike or an unannounced change in parts ordered from a supplier.

Since the most important elements in product development are time and money, the entrepreneur must devise a *schedule*. Check points must be identified, with special emphasis on the more critical check points. If a pilot cannot get his plane to reach critical velocity at the critical time, he must abort takeoff and start again. So, too, must the entrepreneur face his problems and adjust his plans when he fails to meet his check points. Perhaps he will have to give up one product entirely or sell it to another company. Early signs of trouble usually mean there are bigger problems to come. These signs must be heeded.

Amar Bose of Bose Products has said that the symptoms that entrepreneurs and the market call "undercapitalization"—the most frequently cited cause of new business failure—are really inaccurate estimates of costs and time for product development, and the stubborn pursuit of a particular goal despite continued failure to meet cost and time schedules.

5 HOW TO FIND AND ATTRACT YOUR KEY ASSOCIATES

James I. Stockwell *

In Chapters 2 and 3 you read about some of the sensitive issues involved in choosing partners. In this chapter the discussion is broadened to include other key associates. These first-line managers are often as important to the success of your business as your cofounders, and yet they must be persuaded to join your firm with much less of a stock incentive. As you look for these first-line managers, it is important to know where to go for leads, how to interview candidates, and what to offer as salary and other incentives.

Before initiating your search, you should articulate the major elements of your business plan and identify the areas of responsibility into which you will fit your new employees. A well-developed business plan may enable you to entice an able man away from a secure position with a large company. Beyond selling a potential associate on your prospects, it is also important to determine whether he or she will fit the chemistry of your company. Three critical situations in Adage, Inc., illustrate how important a proper fit can be in a small company.

Although I realized that a new business involves risk, I could

* James I. Stockwell received his S.B. in management from M.I.T. He was a founder and senior vice-president and treasurer of Adage, Inc. He is currently a consultant with Heidrick and Struggles, Inc., a firm that specializes in executive recruitment.

not judge my own or my partners' risk orientation until we were about to complete a $2 million financing arrangement. Less than 24 hours before the closing date, our corporate counsel advised us not to close the deal because one potential investor might not prove reliable. He was to have been responsible for $150,000. Within a few hours, another cofounder and I pledged all our ownership in the company as collateral for a loan of $150,000 in order to complete the financing on schedule. As you evaluate prospective partners, try to decide whether they are prepared to meet this kind of challenge.

Do your potential partners share your code of ethics? Shortly after we made our first product deliveries, we were advised by a prospective customer that a buy decision had been made in our favor. The order was firm—except that the customer's purchasing agent wanted us to finance a weekend in New York with a "model" of his choice. We huddled and declined.

What happens when sickness strikes a partner? Our board of directors had to face this issue when I was in line for the presidency of Adage, Inc. At just that time, I learned that I had multiple sclerosis, a disease that is sometimes terminal and for which there is no cure. How much responsibility can a sick person handle? This is a tough issue to face without feelings of guilt and recrimination.

Obviously, you cannot discuss every possible type of crisis with prospective partners to test their reactions. But do not begrudge the time you must spend in screening candidates to get a feel for their flexibility as well as their skills. In every instance you should be forthright about your own goals and about your company's strengths and weaknesses. Do not hold back essential information that might influence a candidate's decision to join your enterprise. And trust your instincts if someone with the right background does not seem personally compatible.

Finding People

Suppose you are looking for a marketing man, a financial specialist, and a foreman. Here are some examples of the type of talent search you might initiate.

1. You and your cofounder are both engineers for a large corporation. Together you have invented a new computer memory device, and now you need a marketing specialist to complete your team.

a. Pick a successful man in one of the smaller companies that will be a competitor. Arrange a meeting, and discuss your plans with him. Ask him if he would be interested in joining you. If he isn't, does he know someone who might be? If he is frustrated in his present job, he may be ready for a change. If he has enjoyed building up his present company and wants to remain, he may want to give a similar opportunity to one of his subordinates or to a friend in a competitor's plant.

b. Talk to a salesman who is familiar with your product, someone you might want to hire when you can afford a full-time salesman. Ask him about his boss's marketing experience and interests. If his boss seems to be the type of person you are looking for, ask the salesman to set up a meeting for you.

c. Visit a supplier for your major source of raw material. He should know marketing men in your field and may be willing to recommend potential associates if he considers you a future customer.

2. You have invented a biodegradable detergent and, together with a marketing man, are ready to form a new company. Neither of you has a business or financial background.

a. Visit a bank where you are known. Talk to a loan officer about your plan, and ask him if he can suggest a financial specialist for your company. If he has no suggestions of his own, ask for the name of a loan officer in a larger bank who might provide leads. (If a bank executive recommends someone whom you eventually hire, you may be on your way to establishing a line of credit.)

b. Contact a member of an accounting firm that prepares audits for a competitor of yours or a company in a similar field. Independent auditing firms are identified in corporate annual reports, which are on file in most business college libraries. Tell your story to the person you have chosen, and ask for leads. There may be a manager or junior manager in his firm who is eager to get into industry.

c. Ask your physician for leads. Since he is probably in a high income bracket, he may know investment bankers or other financiers and may have heard of a financial man looking for a change.

3. You are starting a new company that will make printed circuit boards. You already have financial and marketing experts on your team, but you need a foreman to oversee plating operations.

a. Visit a plant where similar devices are manufactured, in the role of a potential customer. Ask for a tour of the facilities. Take careful note of the best-run facilities. Find out the foreman's name, and call him later on to see if he can give you a contact.

b. Make a "sales call" on a large manufacturer with facilities of his own who may use a small company for specialty runs. Tour the plants, and look for well-organized facilities. Then make your own contacts.

I have purposely left family and friends off the list of prospective associates. I have a strong feeling that the most difficult personnel decisions—to discipline, to change responsibilities, to fire—are too difficult when intimate ties exist between partners or between employer and employee.

Advertising Personnel Needs

In addition to the direct approach described above, consider such free or low-cost sources of information as alumni placement bureaus, professional newsletters, printed notices and signs, state and federal employment agencies, and friends and acquaintances. Every alumni placement bureau has more registrants than it can possibly handle effectively, with attractive positions available in such giants as General Motors, du Pont, and Exxon. But if you take time to describe your business plan and your personnel needs to an alumni placement officer, perhaps over a lunch that you have paid for, you may be introduced to some very talented people. A special-interest story in your alumni bulletin or in a professional newsletter may attract people whom you would not have guessed would be interested in joining a new venture. Be alert to anyone who seems interested in your story. What seems like a casual conversation with a fellow alumnus at an alumni luncheon may indicate a more than casual desire to join your enterprise. Sometimes people just need to be asked.

I have included signs on my list of sources because they are cheap and because you may not be aware of how and where to use them. Many professionals who go to annual conventions are looking for new jobs, and a printed notice or a sign posted on a bulletin board may produce results. There are many other locations to post simple signs: bulletin boards in colleges, churches, lodges, and community centers.

State and federal employment agencies can be helpful in filling a variety of support positions. Within major metropolitan areas, there are a large number of semiskilled personnel whose initial path to employment is through an agency. There is no cost to your company for registering, and most state and federal employment officers will make a great effort to find people for you.

Don't overlook contacts with former classmates, skiing companions, your college professors, or casual acquaintances. If you are convinced of the worth of your enterprise and can communicate your enthusiasm, people will be attracted to you. As you move about, don't hesitate to tell your story. Then be aggressive when you spot talent.

I have purposely reserved the more traditional routes for finding people until the end of this section because I believe that the techniques used to attract key staff should be as exciting and as innovative as your company itself. I also believe that you should spend as little money as possible. But if you can afford them, the established channels include classified ads in newspapers and magazines, personnel agencies, professional recruiters, and management consultants. Costs in each category vary considerably. A local paper reaching 100,000 or fewer readers will carry your 2″ × 2″ ad all week for the same one-time rate charged by a large metropolitan paper for its Sunday edition—approximately $200. Personnel agencies charge 6 to 10 percent of the annual offer you make to a secretary who is actually hired and at least 10 to 15 percent for professional personnel referred to you, if you hire them. Professional recruiters may ask for a nonrefundable deposit of $1000, to be applied against their 15 or 20 percent fee. Top executive search firms will guarantee to find you a qualified person for 25 to 33 percent of starting salary.

Results from each source are not predictable and do not necessarily correlate with cost. A small, carefully composed, and properly timed newspaper ad in the weekly help-wanted section may be more effective than a splashy ad in the Sunday paper. All ads should (1) use a layout technique that will attract the reader's attention; (2) describe enough about the position to make it sound attractive, yet eliminate unqualified applicants; (3) include a few words about what the company does; (4) identify the name of a person to be contacted; and (5) ask for résumés if appropriate. Most large newspapers have someone in their classified departments who will help you design an ad. A tear sheet will be furnished before publication upon request.

Here are some additional guidelines: the "right" person may have missed your ad on its first time around; repeated placement of your ad may be necessary to establish your company's credibility; a short, easily pronounceable (fictitious, if necessary) name as a contact person is more attractive than a difficult name; nonprofessionals do not like to change jobs before vacation periods, Christmas holidays, or year-end bonus payments; Sunday want-ad sections attract a large and varied readership.

The caliber of personnel who own or work for professional agencies, recruiting companies, and management consultant firms ranges from excellent to very poor. As soon as you run your first ad, you will be contacted by several agencies with candidates immediately available to fill all your needs. Before you say, "Send them over," take some time to visit the agencies and discuss the positions more thoroughly. You will find that some are no more than post office boxes. Many will fill your mail box with irrelevant résumés or your office with unqualified candidates. Some, on the other hand, will have specialists in each job category who are experienced in cutting out misfits. This will save you hours of wasted effort. Do not hesitate to call any agency to task if necessary, but only after you have invested some time in describing your needs.

Interviewing and Hiring

After several months of job hunting in 1955, I returned to a small company for a final interview. The vice-president discussed the details of the job and company benefits and then made a firm salary offer—about 40 percent lower than I had anticipated. It would be doubled in twelve months, he said, if I could improve my boss's efficiency by 50 percent during that time. The challenge seemed real, and the opportunity appealed to me. I accepted. Several months passed before I realized that the salary raise hinged on a multitude of unmeasurable criteria, that my expectations would not be realized, and that the same offer had brought a number of people into the company who were now plotting revenge. The lesson is: Don't build up unrealistic expectations to attract capable employees. There will always be repercussions.

Here are some hints for interviewing prospective employees:
- Ask the candidate to describe his previous experience, both strong and weak points.
- Ask for names of references.
- Ask the candidate what his career plans are, what he wants to do for your company, and what he does not want to do.
- Ask for detailed reasons for his moving from his present or last position.
- Inquire about health, family status, availability for extra work, financial requirements.
- Ask some easy questions and some that are tough.
- Define the position you think he would qualify for, its responsibilities, and the salary—both beginning salary and the range you plan if the company grows as expected.
- Discuss your business plan only after you decide that this is someone you really want. Do not waste time on a poor prospect.
- Your interviewing area should have a degree of privacy consistent with the information to be discussed.
- Ask for samples of the candidate's work.
- Follow up your first interview by doing at least a telephone check on the references. Find out if the references can corroborate the candidate's history.

Here are some pitfalls to avoid:
- Do not spend most of the interview justifying yourself or your business.
- Do not interrupt the candidate to express your own views once he starts talking about himself; the point of the interview is to have him talk freely.
- Do not paint an overly optimistic picture of the company's future.
- Do not overdramatize the magnitude of the task at hand.
- Do not pick a time for the interview when you are likely to be interrupted frequently.
- Do not introduce the candidate to your associates unless there is a good possibility that he will join your company.
- Do not keep a candidate dangling.
- Do not call a candidate's former or present employer without his consent.
- Do not submit the candidate to a bevy of professional tests to determine his qualifications for the job.

Once you have decided to hire a candidate, there are several things to do:
- Make a fair salary offer, consistent with your ability to pay and his financial needs.
- Clearly define what benefits (if any) you are providing for the founders and key employees and which of these will be available to the candidate.
- Define in a letter the salary and benefits and the general area of job responsibility.
- Make an offer on a monthly (not annual) basis.
- Establish a deadline by which the candidate must accept or reject the offer.
- Make the offer contingent upon a medical report that substantiates the candidate's statements about his health.

There are also several things to avoid:

- Do not pad the salary offer with future benefits that may never materialize.
- Do not promise benefits, stock, or options that require stockholder approval, since it may not be forthcoming.
- Do not promise a title that depends on the company's future performance.
- Do not make the offer contingent upon a tight employment contract; this does not work in small companies.
- Do not make a salary offer that is 20 to 40 percent higher than what he is currently getting just to get him on board.
- Do not agree to a host of restrictive conditions (such as insurance, stock ownership, special working hours, bonuses) unless you are willing to grant them to future employees of similar status.

Some of the suggestions listed here are derived from my own and my associates' mistakes. For example, an entrepreneur engaged a management consultant to locate a marketing vice-president. When the consultant in confidence came up with the entrepreneur's college roommate's business partner, he could not resist a telephone call: "Say, Sam, I hear your partner is looking for a job." He never saw the candidate, of course, and it took quite a few drinks to unruffle the consultant's feathers. Another example: an applicant from the West Coast was reluctant to answer my questions about his financial status. He finally assured me that I had nothing to worry about since he had been through personal bankruptcy only twice and that the whole process was worked out very fairly each time. In each case, he had been allowed to retain one car, one television set, and one department store charge account without penalty. I looked further for a business manager for our West Coast organization. A third example: an entrepreneur found a compatible partner, and his company passed through the break-even point. Then, without warning, his partner was totally disabled by a disease that could have been detected prior to start-up of the company. A medical examination for each partner would have been a good investment.

Finding the right people for your company is a tough assignment. Interviewing requires certain skills, and failure to do a thorough job may lead to trouble. There is no such thing as asking too many questions. Often, one key question will bring out unexpected information that you need to make a decision. Develop a list of questions that will probe many aspects of a candidate's personality and background. Keep plugging away until you are satisfied that you have found the right person.

When a person seems right for your company, take advantage of all the information you have gathered about him to persuade him to accept your offer. Explain your business plan, identify the key people who are already part of the plan, and discuss the unfilled jobs. Show the candidate how his skills meet your needs. You should be very matter-of-fact and straightforward, and at the same time you should let him know that you have given a great deal of thought to his role. If you truly believe he will find personal satisfaction in the job you are offering, let him know that. After making a salary offer, suggest that he talk over the opportunity with his family before making a decision. If you have done a good job, his acceptance should be forthcoming within a few days. One final note: once he has accepted, send him a letter confirming the position, the salary, and the starting date. Let him know how pleased you are about his decision to join your enterprise.

Salary

As mentioned earlier, the initial salary for an employee should take into account your ability to pay and his financial needs. Your cofounders and key associates should be able to start out with smaller sums than they would earn in an established company. In fact, the company may not be able to survive without such sacrifices on their part. This cannot go on indefinitely, however. Your business plan should include bringing salaries into line with industry standards at an early date, no more than 18 months after start-up if possible. On the other hand, there is plenty of time to pay yourself a top salary *after* the profit mark has been achieved.

There are several excellent sources for salary information, and it is important to keep up to date. For a minimal cost the U.S. Department of Labor will send you periodic revisions of the National Professional Survey, the Regional Salary Survey, and the Policy and Benefits Survey. If these data are too generalized for your needs, use more specific guidelines, such as Prentice-Hall's Survey of Personnel Policies and Procedures, American Management Association surveys, professional personnel association surveys (for example, surveys of the Electronics Personnel Association); and studies by private reporting services. Most of these reports are available through association membership or by subscription. They cost from $100 to $200 a year for each service.

What about compensation in lieu of salary, such as stock options? My own opinion is that the salary you pay should stand on its own, producing a fair income stream to keep your employee's family stable and to provide savings against future needs. If your key people are fighting a constant battle to make ends meet because they are accepting far less than they need or previously earned, they cannot make the emotional and physical commitment you need from them to make your enterprise work. The difference between success and failure may depend, at some point of crisis, on your employees' willingness to take a 30 percent salary cutback for six to 12 months. This is impossible to carry through if you are paying only 75 percent of the going rate to start with. I believe in avoiding gimmicks and in trying to provide full salaries whenever possible.

Vacations, Holidays, and Sick Leave

There just are not any holidays in the beginning of start-up, unless you count Sundays as holidays. Later on, you should be able to celebrate national and state legal holidays (unless you obtain a working permit from your local police). These add up to about nine a year. I try to use discretion in the choice of holidays recognized each year, selecting those which result in long weekends fairly well distributed throughout the year. Vacation practices are more or less standardized: one week's paid vacation after 12 full months of employment and one additional day for each additional full year, up to a three- or four-week maximum. My own feeling is that all employees should take vacations. Only in an extreme emergency should pay be given instead of vacation. For the sake of efficiency, it is usually best to have everyone on vacation at the same time.

Policy governing sick leave has become almost as standard as vacation and holiday policy. Try to keep accurate and up-to-date records of employees' absences for illness. Although *you* will not take any sick leave, adopt a policy whereby each employee earns one half day of sick leave with pay for each month of employment, up to a maximum account of one month's pay. If serious illness does strike an employee, his accrual of time will give him a means of income, and you will be saved a lot of time trying to decide what is fair.

Insurance

You should have group medical insurance for yourself and your employees. Start as soon as your company qualifies. This may be immediately upon incorporation. Rates vary according to geographic location and the experience of the group to which you are assigned. When your company employs 100 to 150 people, you will get your own particular rating, based on the experience of your company. (So don't process every nuisance claim!) For a reference point, our 1971 rates in Massachusetts were approximately $20 a month for an individual and $50 a month for family coverage. You may want each person to pay his own premium at the beginning; then gradually move to half and half, or the company paying all. It is wise to include major medical coverage, but do not let rates climb sky-high by insuring for all possible risks.

Life insurance in a company group plan is not as important as accident and health insurance for the start-up company, but it is an attractive option when your company can qualify. Rates vary widely, depending on the average age of the group insured. Rates in the range of $.30 to $.50 a month per $1000 of coverage are typical in younger groups. Life insurance may seem like gilding the lily, but we have had three sudden deaths in our company. We purchase life insurance coverage equal to employees' annual salaries, and employees may add up to twice their annual salaries. In one case, we had to convince our thirty-eight-year-old purchasing agent not to cancel his extra coverage. He complained that he couldn't afford the premium payments and that he had never been sick in the ten years he had been with us. Six months later he died of a stroke while on a business trip. His insurance proceeds were the only assets he left behind for his wife and two young sons. My principal concern about insurance is not the amount of coverage but rather that there be at least some coverage. The dollar cost for minimum coverage will give your employees more security than the 5 percent salary increase you might consider instead.

Stock Ownership Plan

One of the exciting aspects of a new company can be the growth in value of its securities. Participation in ownership and the chance to "make a bundle" are factors that draw people from relatively secure positions into a new company. You should establish a set of guidelines whereby the top performers, by any criteria you wish to designate, may have a chance to participate in stock benefits. On the other hand, beyond the founders, ownership should be a benefit and *not* a substitute for fair and equitable compensation. After the 1970 recession in the aerospace and electronic fields, employee stockholders saw the asset base they had built up through stock options deteriorate. In selecting the plan that best fits your company, consider the following:

• Stock ownership requires an investment. Any plan you set up must be reasonable in terms of disposable income.
• If you are not planning a public offering for your company's stock, there will be a limited market for the sale of shares when an employee wants to sell.
• Most sales will be on a restricted basis; that is, the employees must retain ownership for at least two years or face resale on a "letter stock" basis at 40 to 50 percent off market prices.
• There is no need to hand out all the ownership right away. A plan providing for periodic sales may be the best for the employees and the company.
• There is a salary threshold below which stock ownership provides little or no incentive.

Any plan you select must receive stockholder approval and also requires Internal Revenue Service approval if the shares purchased are to qualify for capital gains tax status. The complexities of stock purchase and option plans should be entrusted to your legal counsel. Here is a brief description of three types of plan.

1. *Employee Stock Purchase Plan.* Stock is sold directly to employees on the same basis as to founders or on some adjusted ratio. You will have to set an arbitrary price. This type of plan lets everyone in on the ground floor, gives the company some cash, and calls for a firm investment commitment from employees. Employees take the same risk as the founders, but they do not stand to gain as much because of their limited participation in ownership.

2. *Restricted Stock Option Plan (Qualified or Nonqualified).* Options are granted to employees which give them the right to purchase a certain number of shares at a fixed price, with the option to be exercised in specific increments over five years. The plan is "restricted" in that shares must be held for a certain minimum period before resale. The term "qualified" refers to the tax status of gains or losses on eventual resale. Qualified plans are eligible for capital gains exemptions; nonqualified plans are subject to regular income tax requirements. These plans can pave the way for ownership without any mandatory investment until the employee wishes to buy the stock. But if he waits until the end of five years to exercise his option and then observes the two-year holding period (in the absence of a public stock offering), his near-term gains will be small. If the stock price fluctuates and does not rise above the option price at the end of five years, or if it drops after the investment is made, the employee has waited for nothing.

3. *Phantom Stock Option Plan.* This is similar to the restricted stock option plan, but, in fact, no shares ever change hands. The company, working with an investment banker, designs a plan to measure what the value of company stock would be at any given time if it were being traded on the open market. (In a more advanced stage of the company's growth, there may actually be a market for your stock.) Employees are granted "phantom" shares equivalent to actual shares, but subsequent transactions are with the company instead of a public buyer.

No stock changes hands, and the employee ends up with a cash payment from the company at the time he wishes to sell or when he terminates employment. This payment is equal to the amount he would have earned had he actually purchased shares. This type of plan is attractive if a fair valuation is put on the stock. Often, however, valuation is more conservative than the price that the public may set in open trading.

Each of the plans outlined above may be tailored to fit your company's needs. Provisions may be added to cover conditions of employment, noncompetition agreements, company-funded purchases, guarantees with respect to resale, and guarantees covering future registration if and when the company goes public. It is essential that your attorney help you draw up your plan. Whatever plan you choose should enable you to grant key personnel meaningful ownership positions. Be sure that top performers are being suitably rewarded and are thus motivated to continue their performance.

The amount of stock ownership made available to associates through direct sale or option should be related to the total capital structure of your company at any given time. If you receive outside financing, your stockholders may be willing to approve a plan under which options equal to 10 percent of the outstanding (not authorized) shares are granted to full-time employees. One method of controlling stock distribution is to set a limit for each employee, based on a multiple of option price times the number of shares granted. For a nonofficer, this should be equal to salary. For officers, it should be equal to a low multiple of salary. Usually, the first grant represents at least a $1000 investment.

The guidelines for an overall plan are easier to establish than the exact percentage of stock ownership granted to founders and other key associates. The range is large and is dependent on the company's capital structure. Here are some typical situations.

1. You are a technical man with a unique idea and have found two other partners to participate in a start-up. How much stock should each of you receive? If your business plan requires $300,000 in outside capital, you may have to give 30 percent equity to your investors and be able to hold another 10 percent aside for second-round financing. You may also want to reserve 10 percent for future key personnel. As the principal founder, you may reasonably expect some edge over your partners in dividing the balance. The result could be:

30 percent—financial backers
10 percent—reserved for second-round financing
10 percent—reserved for future key employees
20 percent—yourself
15 percent—number 2 founder
15 percent—number 3 founder

This distribution is only one of several possibilities. You may want to give all the partners equal equity, ignore future employees until the company refinances on a successful profit record, negotiate a better deal with your investors, or have each partner participate in the initial financing.

2. Your company is well into the start-up phase, the necessary capital has been raised, and you are building your team. You find an ideal production man who will probably not become an officer. Should you offer him equity for joining the company? I think not. This is the type of key employee who should be included in the stock option plan you adopt after your company has established some sort of track record.

3. After 18 months your company has not achieved the break-even point as anticipated. It is clear that the founding group lacks a salesman. The best man available is a vice-president in a successful competitor's organization. How much ownership should you offer him in trying to persuade him to join you? Since your company may not make it without him and your total investment would then be lost, you may have to

offer him from 10 to 25 percent ownership. Making this available will be a problem for *all* your stockholders—financial backers, founders, and other owners or option holders.

Profit-Sharing Plans

In the first years of start-up, you cannot spend the time or money to set up profit-sharing plans. If you are looking ahead, however, think in terms of a maximum tax-free corporate contribution of 15 percent of pretax profits. These dollars can be paid out immediately as taxable income, with the distribution based on some combination of salary and years of service. As an alternative, the funds can be invested in a profit-sharing trust, with or without matching employee contributions. For this type of plan, no tax need be paid by the employee until the investment is paid over to him. If this plan is tied into a pension plan, payment will be made upon his retirement.

Expense Accounts

Expense accounts should be set up to provide straightforward reimbursement of actual expenses incurred. They should not be used to compensate a partner or employee for an inadequate salary. In today's charge-card economy, there is no need to issue very much cash for traveling or entertaining. Have each person fill out an expense report (available from a business stationery supplier) and clip the charge receipts to it. These can then be matched with the monthly charge account billings. With a reasonable effort, expense accounting will take care of itself. You will have to develop norms for mileage and out-of-pocket expenses. You may want to call on your auditor for help in setting limits. Use some discretion in issuing charge cards to employees or to new salesmen. Several months after discharging a relatively new, nonproductive salesman, we were still trying to determine how many flowers, clothes, and other purchases he had charged to our account.

Commissions and Bonuses

A commission or bonus plan may be just right for your product or market area. For most technically based companies, however, there is usually no compelling reason to use this type of compensation during the start-up phase. Founders and other key associates are highly motivated and will do their best without bonuses. When your company is doing well, provide some ownership as a bonus. Later on, relate bonuses to the achievement of specific performance goals. As soon as you are large enough to establish a sales department, and after one or two years to measure your company's sales performance, commissions should begin to account for the top 20 percent of salesmen's compensation.

Personnel Relations

Your newly hired staff—key associates and others—will have a strong sense of identification with your enterprise. For this reason, you might expect turnover to be quite low. In fact, the pressure-tank atmosphere of a new business results in a high rate of turnover. The norm in the electronics industry is 2 percent a month, or about 25 percent a year. For a start-up venture, 30 to 40 percent should be anticipated. This can be controlled if you have an "early warning system." Holding on to your people as your enterprise grows is more directly related to *communication* than to any other single factor. If your objectives are being achieved and those responsible know their work is appreciated, they will usually stay with the company. If the communication process breaks down and you stop listening or looking for early signs of trouble, your employees will look elsewhere for more responsive leadership.

At one stage in my company's growth, I decided that communication should be improved. I set up a series of meetings with groups of approximately 20 people to discuss the very difficult position the company was in, the extent of our losses, the necessity for stringent expense control, and the probability of a personnel cutback. At the conclusion of one such meeting, I had the feeling that my message was not getting across. I pressed for questions. There were two, each having to do with the number of shares of stock that might be made available to employees if and when the company went public. Sometimes people do not want to hear what you are saying, especially if the news is bad. Nevertheless, you must keep people informed of your plans, your hopes, and your problems, or they will look elsewhere for a more responsive environment.

Job satisfaction and motivation depend to a great extent on ego satisfaction. If, for some reason, an employee is not satisfied with your response to his performance, all the benefits in the world will not keep him on your team. Someone put it this way: "How popular would bowling be if you never saw the pins fall?" People want to know how they are doing. You should work out a method of measuring your own and your employees' performance so that each person will gain a sense of satisfaction when goals are met. This is difficult to do during start-up when tasks overlap and victories are few. Everyone gets discouraged when things go wrong, whether it is a nonfunctioning breadboard, a refusal from a bank loan officer, or a cold shoulder from a potential customer. The entrepreneur cannot make everybody happy all the time. But before staff turnover becomes a problem, let your employees know how much you appreciate their work.

In addition to financial compensation for performance there are also some things with no dollar significance that can make your company a very pleasant place to work. You should take advantage of your company's size and flexibility to grant reasonable requests from your employees without worrying about setting precedents. Don't be afraid to change work schedules from time to time to accommodate special plans—a Friday afternoon off for skiing or sailing—or to let your employees choose their own mode of dress or office decor. Many capable people join start-up companies just because they feel stifled by the inflexibility of large corporations. During start-up, your openness to individual needs and personal taste will help to make up for the lack of more tangible benefits.

There is no magic way to find and attract staff, but the task can be simplified if you do the following:

• Develop a solid business plan.
• Be aggressive in your search.
• Compensate fairly, avoiding extremes.
• Keep communication paths open, and provide performance feedback.

II FINANCIAL CONSIDERATIONS

During the earliest phases of start-up you must build up enough psychological momentum to carry you through the next several difficult years. Few of the rewards of being in business for yourself come during this initial period. What is often an early requirement, seeking funding for your venture, will require great courage. The next three chapters present different viewpoints prevalent in venture funding. John Windle is in a unique position: he is a founder of his own company and also active in the process of providing funds for entrepreneurs. John Stuart is a "100 percent entrepreneur." His chapter will tell you a great deal about the difficult, and seemingly endless, process of seeking money. Dan Holland is a full-time venture capitalist from one of the country's most prestigious firms. His chapter will give you a very good idea of what negotiations for money include and what the venture capitalist is looking for.

In raising money at the beginning, you may feel that you are at a disadvantage since your company is not yet off the ground. Remember, however, that you have two strong points in your favor. First, investors make their money by discovering new ideas and talent. They need you just as much as you need them. Second, you are probably not desperate for money in the first round. Your business is not about to close. Time is on your side; you can keep looking for other sources if you are turned down or if the deal is not right.

Once you have found one or more interested investors, a stage of quasi-negotiation begins. A number of strategies are recommended for the negotiations, often from two opposing points of view: the investor's and the entrepreneur's. As an entrepreneur, I believe you should fight to retain every percentage point of equity that you can. The first funding in your company is only the beginning. Every time you raise additional funds, you will have to give up more equity. If you do not give up too much in the beginning, you will have what you need later. Somewhere along the way you will encounter an investor who asks "What do you care how much you give up as long as you make your million dollars?" Your answer should be "If it doesn't make any difference, why don't you take a little less and I will take a little more?" There is another type of investor who says he can "do a deal in a day" and wants you to let him consider your situation on an exclusive basis for a few weeks. Tell him that you cannot let him consider it exclusively but that there are only one or two others who are considering it at the same time; that is, he need not worry that he will have the deal scooped from under him after he has made his investigation. This will enable you to find a suitable investor sometime before you are eligible for Social Security.

You will meet some investors who believe that an entrepreneur should sink all his own assets into his venture so that he will be fully motivated to make it a success. I believe that such an arrangement is a serious mistake. When the company gets into a little financial trouble and has to withhold salary for a time, your personal financial condition will quickly take precedence over company problems, and the company will suffer. You should retain at least enough of your own funds to ride out difficult periods during start-up.

Finally, in your negotiations for money remember that there is absolutely no correlation between the amount of money you ask for and the percentage of equity you must give up. Most venture capitalists have certain rules of thumb: they want 20 or 35 or 51 percent of every deal they make, whether it is for $100,000 or $1 million. So if you need $150,000 but think $200,000 would make the deal less risky, make your case for the larger sum. It will not cost you more in terms of equity. Some investors will ask you to cite the smallest amount of money you could get by on as well as the amount you would prefer. They will then give you the lesser amount, with a promise of more if you reach certain early milestones. For this reason it is a good idea to have at least a little slack in your estimate of funding requirements for bargaining purposes.

These are my own opinions. The next three chapters will give you some others.

William D. Putt

6 THE FINANCIAL PROPOSAL
John P. Windle*

The problem with most financial proposals is not in the way they are written but in the business plan on which they are based. In many start-up proposals, it appears that the entrepreneur has tried to anticipate what the investor wants to see and, in doing so, has failed to think through his business plan thoroughly. For example, in a recent situation, the principals of a new software company had projected that within three years their company would grow to $5 million in sales and $400,000 in net income. Under questioning by a prospective investor, it became apparent that the principals had chosen these figures, not because they really believed them, but because they thought they were what the investor *wanted to hear*. As you might have guessed, the principals had no luck with this investor or any others until they reworked their proposal to put it on a more substantial basis.

There are many ways of saying what must be said in order to induce investors to put their money into a new business. At least three elements seem to be essential:
1. An opportunity
2. A plan for how you will exploit that opportunity
3. The talent to execute your plan

* John P. Windle received his S.B. degree in electrical engineering and his S.M. in management from M.I.T. In 1969 he was a founder of Business Equities Corporation. He is currently president of BEC Consulting Group, Inc.

These elements will be discussed in later sections of this chapter. However, before considering guidelines for preparing a proposal, let us examine the uses of a financial proposal.

Reasons for Having a Financial Proposal

The primary purpose of the financial proposal is, of course, to help you in encouraging investors to put money into your business. It will also serve other important uses: a planning document for yourself, descriptive material for financial intermediaries, and an information document for your advisors. Finally, once you have your money, it will help you to get moving quickly.

In its primary purpose, the financial proposal is the major document for potential investors and lenders. In many cases an investor will decide whether or not to work further with you on the basis of this document alone. (In other cases an investor will prefer to make this decision on the basis of a telephone conversation or a brief face-to-face meeting with you or your intermediary.) Since the financial proposal is used in this way, it should be a selling document—but it should not be an overselling document—for your company.

Once you have passed through the investor's initial screening, the proposal becomes a tool for assisting and speeding the investor's evaluation of your new venture. In a situation we worked on recently several entrepreneurs with an interesting concept, but a weak financial proposal, found that investors were taking two to three months just to give a preliminary decision. They had developed a unique process that they thought would help contractors of multistory housing units to save substantial time in one of the essential steps in construction. The most notable gap in their original proposal was that it made no estimate of the value of the process to contractors, except to say that it was "believed to be very valuable." In order to solve the problem, we surveyed contractors, explained the process to them, and got them to estimate the cost savings they would realize. Once this information was added to the proposal, the entrepreneurs found that investors were able to make decisions on their proposal in a fraction of the time it previously took.

In addition to using the financial proposal to evaluate your company, investors will use it to evaluate you. Investors will be trying to gauge your ability to plan and to think things through as they read your proposal. (A fuller discussion of the criteria investors use is included in Chapters 7 and 8.)

The use of the financial proposal as a business plan for yourself is almost as important as its use in dealing with investors. It will probably be the only plan you will have in the early months of the venture. As such, you should use it as a method of simulating the business. By thinking through and recording what you must do to exploit your opportunity and what consequences are likely to result, you should be able to work out the bugs, spot the critical items, and integrate the major activities.

One tip here: State what you will do in a way that can be measured. A proposal we worked on recently included the statement "In our initial marketing efforts, our principals will contact representative customer companies in each of our major market segments." This is so vague it probably applies to all new ventures and therefore says nothing. As reworked, the statement spelled out which segments would be covered, how many companies would be contacted in each, who would contact them, by when, and what results were expected. Backup material included a complete schedule for this critical marketing work.

Stating what you can do in a way that can be measured will help you to learn whether you are making the progress you should be making. It will also help your investors to determine whether or not what you say is valid. You might prefer that your investors trust your statements instead of validating them, but most sophisticated investors will not move without validating key statements. Thus any help you give them will just speed up a process that would take place anyway.

Your financial proposal will be useful in contacts with many people in a position to help your enterprise. One of these uses is to help you deal with intermediaries. The proposal will help potential intermediaries to quickly assess your intentions and to determine whether or not they can help you. It will further help them to decide which investors to approach on your behalf. On your side of the coin, the proposal will enable you to get an evaluation of your business from the intermediary and thus help you to correct problems and do any necessary rethinking.

Your financial proposal will also give other professional advisors, such as attorneys, accountants, and perhaps consultants, a picture of your business. You may want to use parts of the proposal to encourage vendors to work with you. One entrepreneur I know says he had to go through a basic explanation of his business five to ten times a month in the early months. A written proposal can save you a lot of time by avoiding this repeated effort.

All of the uses mentioned thus far are ways the proposal will help you before you get your money. Once you have your money, a good proposal—or, more specifically, the business plan embodied in a good proposal—becomes more, not less, important. Often start-up companies that don't have a good plan waste a lot of time and money deciding how to use the money they have received. Thus one of the most important uses of the proposal is to ensure that you get off to a fast start and are pointed in the right direction as soon as you receive your money.

The Major Financial Issues

The major financial issues in your proposal will include how much money to seek now, how much of your company to give up for the money, and how to package the deal. How to package the deal will be covered in Chapter 8; this section will focus on the first two issues.

How Much Money Should You Ask For Now?
There is no easy answer to this question, but there are several ways to approach an answer. The most basic approach is to prepare projected financial statements. One of the most difficult steps in compiling your pro forma financial statements may be the projection of your sales volume. There are, however, techniques to help you. One such technique is to make a model of your business and simulate the model to a point in the future. For example, your model might include the number of salesmen or distributors you will have, the number of accounts each will call on, the percentage of these accounts that can be converted to customers, and the frequency and size of orders from each customer. By making different assumptions for each of the variables and seeing how realistic and acceptable the results are, you can obtain a reasonable estimate of your sales. Once you have projected your level of sales, estimate your various costs and capital expenditures by thinking through what is necessary to support the level of sales. Then relate your cash inflows to the necessary cash outflows. The excess of outflows over inflows should then give you an estimate of how much money you will need.

Once you have determined your cash needs according to your plan, you should allow for slippages and unforeseen contingencies. Even in well-planned start-ups slippages and contingencies often increase the cash requirement substantially. Knowing this, some entrepreneurs ask for 50 to 100 percent more cash than they really need. This may sound good in theory, but we've found that most investors, perhaps wisely, won't put up money for unknown uses. If you want to put in a contingency, keep it in the 10 to 20 percent range.

After you project your cash needs on the basis just described, it's a good idea to check it by another approach. See how your requirements compare with roughly similar start-up situations that are a few years ahead of you. You can find out how much money others got in several ways. The simplest is to call the presidents of recent new ventures—you probably will be surprised by their willingness to help. You can also ask your intermediary, if you're using one, and you can examine the prospectuses of companies that have recently gone public to see how much early money they got.

In determining how much to ask for, you should not be shortsighted. Project your requirements for at least the first three to five years. This will enable you to do a couple of useful things. First, it will give you a basis for considering how much of your requirement to ask for now and how much to ask for later. The more you get now, the more you'll probably have to pay for it, but if you don't get enough now, you may run the risk of going bankrupt or having to go back to investors in a desperate situation.

A second advantage you get from knowing your requirements over three to five years is that it gives you the opportunity to try to make at least contingent provisions for having additional money available when you need it.

How Much of Your Company Should You Give Up to Get Your Money?
Here again there are no clear-cut answers, but there are useful approaches.

Here is a way of making a first cut:

1. Project the future performance of your company to a point

when it could go public. Typically, this means $200,000 to $500,000 of net profit after tax. Do this on three bases: optimistic, pessimistic, and most likely.

2. Project the market value at that future point. You can do this by applying the price/earnings ratio of companies similar to yours that are already public. You will probably find this will fall in the range of 10 to 30 for a price/earnings multiple, though it will depend on the type of company and will fluctuate with the ups and downs of the stock market.

3. Set the price of the stock you will sell to raise capital so that investors will get an adequate return if they invest (buy stock) now and sell it in the future when you are public. Keep in mind that the investors probably won't be able to sell their stock until your company has been public for several years. During the period in which they can't sell, the investors probably will value the stock at a much lower price/earnings multiple than the stock market. For example, if your stock is selling at a 30-times multiple, investors may value stock that they hold but cannot sell at a 15- to 20-times multiple.

Estimates vary widely on what return is considered adequate, but most investors probably look for 30 to 60 percent annual compounded rate of return. Or, in other words, they want about two to four times their money back if they get it back in three years, or four to ten times if they get it back in five years. These rates may seem shockingly high compared to the 5 percent or so you get on your savings. But remember that, even though your venture seems great to you, you'll probably admit it's a lot riskier than a savings bank. And even many successful investors end up with an appreciation of only 10–12 percent a year on their money after they average out those situations that did return 30–60 percent with those that folded.

Once you have priced your stock using the above method, it's a good idea to check what you're giving up against what has happened in other situations. The sources referred to in discussing how much money to ask for should also be helpful here.

Two final points: First, there is a relation between what you ask others to put in and what you yourself put in. One entrepreneur who had a personal net worth of about $100,000 planned to put only $20,000 of this into his new venture. He was asking investors to put in $250,000. Prospective investors told him that if he had so little faith in his own business, they weren't interested. Thus the venture never got off the ground. Investors like to see that the entrepreneur is wholly committed to the success of his business. As a way of ensuring this commitment, they expect the entrepreneur to put a high percentage of his own net worth into the business.

Second, once you get your money, be very careful of what my partner, Dick Koplow, likes to call "Parkinson's Law of Venture Capital." This "law" says that financial requirements expand to use up all the available capital. If you are fortunate enough to get a cushion over and above what you really need, plan not to use it, and make sure you don't use it unless you really have to.

Some Tough Procedural Issues

The procedural issues of how to write your proposal shouldn't be difficult, and they shouldn't take time away from the hard work of planning your venture. But in practice many entrepreneurs get hung up on procedural questions, for example,
1. Who should actually write the proposal?
2. How honest should it be?
3. How comprehensive should it be?

Who Should Write Your Proposal?
If your answer to this question is basically "I'm the entrepreneur, and I have to write it," then you can safely skip to the

next question. Although most proposals are probably written by the entrepreneur involved, a fair number are written by intermediaries, lawyers, or consultants. I believe you do yourself a disservice if you have someone else do the basic work of writing your proposal for you. Whoever does the basic work will see a lot of issues in the process and will have the best understanding of the proposal once it is written. I think these benefits should accrue to the entrepreneur, not to his advisors. In addition, by doing the basic proposal writing yourself, you learn how good you are at business planning and how well you like this important entrepreneurial task. If you're not good at it or don't like it, this may be a sign you should reconsider whether you want to start your own business.

Once you have done the basic work of planning the venture and putting the plan on paper, you should review it, spot problems, make changes as necessary, and then finally polish the organization and writing. In the latter tasks, I think outside help can be much more productive. An independent review of the proposal by someone with different blind spots from yours, and possibly with new creative inputs, can be most valuable. And if you need and can afford outside help in polishing the writing, then this may be worthwhile.

How Honest Should I Be in Writing the Proposal?
Moral questions aside, even from a strictly pragmatic point of view, I think the answer is that you should be honest. If you try to overstate your opportunities or hide some of your problems, the chances are you'll get picked up on at least part of what you're trying to hide. Once this happens, the damage to your credibility is far worse than having shown a little less opportunity or a little greater risk. Hiding things also prevents you from asking for help on them. One of your advisors may have a great solution for a hard problem, but you'll never discover this unless you are open about your needs.

In being honest, however, you should not be unduly conservative or pessimistic. Present your opportunities. But, in being
honest, also point out the key turning points or risks you will
encounter in realizing your opportunities.

How Comprehensive Should I Be?

Here, I think, you will have to consider some trade-offs. If your
document is too skimpy, you will find that even if investors are
interested, they will keep coming back to you with questions
and will take a long time to make a decision. On the other
hand, if it is too long, you run the risk that the prospective
investor may never read it at all, and you will also spend a lot
of time writing, rewriting, and updating it.

I think the guideline here is to emphasize materiality,
organization, and quality, but not length. You should probably
have three levels of detail.

1. A *summary*—not just a list of topics, but a summary that hits
the key points and can be read by an investor in no more than
120 seconds. Some people like to call this a miniproposal and
may send it out by itself as a first step. In any case it is very
important and useful.

2. The *proposal*—20 to 30 double-spaced pages of text and
maybe five to ten pages of financial statements and pro formas.

3. *Sufficient backup material*—material that does not go with the
original proposal but from which you can readily provide
answers or more detail if asked. You will probably find it useful
to organize this material in a loose-leaf notebook complete with
a table of contents and tabs, so that, even under pressure, you
can quickly and easily find exactly what you are looking for.

Risks and Shaky Evidence

At the beginning of this chapter, I said there are three things
you must have to interest investors: an opportunity, a plan to

exploit that opportunity, and the talent to execute your plan. These are things that turn investors on. There are two things that turn them off: unreasonable risks and shaky evidence.

Every new venture has risks. Few entrepreneurs adequately cope with these risks, and some entrepreneurs ignore the risks altogether. In order to cope adequately with the risks in your venture, you first have to identify them. This seems to be very difficult for entrepreneurs to do, primarily, I suspect, for psychological reasons. One method that may help you is to set aside a specific two- to three-hour period during which you focus only on identifying risks. You should probably also ask your team members and advisors to tell you the risks they see.

Once you have identified the risks, you should calibrate them by estimating how likely each is to materialize and how badly it would hurt if it did. For the more serious risks, you should try to work out ways of protecting your company against them.

Once you have done your homework on risks, the question arises What, if anything, should you say in your proposal about risks? This is particularly important since the degree of risk is one of the main criteria that investors use in determining whether to invest and what percentage of the company to ask for. Most proposals omit an explicit discussion of the risks involved in a situation, and many advisors agree with this approach, saying that to tell investors about risks just gives them reasons for saying no. I would argue against this position for several reasons. First, discussing your risks increases your credibility. Every venture capital investor knows there are risks in all new ventures. If you take this approach, you become more believable. Second, an indication that you have identified, calibrated, and developed fixes for your risks helps demonstrate your skill as a manager. Third, an open discussion of risks gives you the opportunity to demonstrate that they're not as serious as the investor might first have thought.

Besides unreasonable risks, investors are often troubled by

shaky evidence. Sometimes an entrepreneur says in effect "I know this will work. Do I have to prove it?" I think the answer is generally yes. One of the basic questions here is what constitutes evidence. It may be useful to think of a hierarchy of evidence. Take, for example, the question "Can you sell your product?" The hierarchy here might be as follows:

1. Shipments which have been accepted and are satisfactory
2. Orders without cancellation clauses
3. Orders with cancellation clauses
4. Letters of intent
5. Favorable reaction to the product—written
6. Favorable reaction to the product—oral
7. Logical reasoning showing why people will buy
8. The existence of a market

Similar hierarchies could be worked out for other important questions.

I think it is safe to say that coping with your risks and getting your evidence in place will markedly improve your chances of success.

What Should Be Included in the Financial Proposal?

This section describes what should go into the proposal both from the point of view of supplying the information investors need and from the point of view of serving you as a business plan. The items included are distilled from several hundred proposals we've looked at and the comments investors have made on them. The format is that of an annotated checklist of what should go into a proposal.

Outline for a Financial Proposal
I.   Summary
        As mentioned earlier, this should not be a mere listing of
        topics but should hit the high points of your proposal.

II.   Table of Contents
III. Company Description
      A. What business are you in?
      B. What are your chief
         1. Products or services?
         2. Customers?
         3. Applications?
      C. What is your distinctive competence? (What are the chief factors that will account for your success?)

      Here you should give the investor a clear picture of what you're up to and give him good reasons for believing you will succeed. If you are entering a competitive field (and most are), the distinctive competence description becomes very important. In any case a distinctive competence must be related to a need. Examples that I've seen (stated informally) include the following:
      • "Our machine is much faster and the customer needs speed."
      • "Our machine requires little operator training, and operator training on competitive machines has been a big problem to the customer."
      • "Our software technology makes it easy for a customer to convert from his existing system to ours, and conversion has been one of the industry's major problems."
      • "We will be the lowest cost entry in a market that is very price sensitive."
      • "We have very strong relationships with customers that order $16 million a year, and our product (or service) is at least as good as the competition."

IV.   Market Analysis and Marketing
      A. Industry description and outlook

1. What industry are you in?
2. How big is it now? How big will it be in five years? ten years?
3. What are its chief characteristics?
4. Who are or will be the major customers?
5. What are or will be the major applications?
6. What are the major trends in the industry?

The importance of this section on industry description and outlook varies according to how large your venture will be in relation to the industry you're in. If you will be very small, say less than 1 percent of the industry, you probably can omit it entirely or treat it briefly. If you are larger and do include it, you should check to see that it is not redundant with sections that follow.

B. Target markets
  1. What are the major market segments you will penetrate?
  2. For each major segment
    a. What are the dollar and unit sales (for the whole segment and for your company)?
    b. Who are the major customers?
    c. What are the major applications?
    d. What are the products or services to be sold?
    e. What is the profitability of each?
  3. For each major application, what are the following:
    a. Requirements of the customer?
    b. Current ways of filling these requirements?
    c. Buying habits of the customer?
    d. Impact on the customer of using your product or service?
      (i) User economics (How much will it save him per year? What return on investment will he get?)

(ii) Other impact (Will he have to change his way of doing things? Buy other equipment? Change work habits?)

C. Competition
  1. What companies will you compete with (including those like you, who are not yet in the market)?
  2. How do you compare with other companies?
  3. What competiton will you meet in each product or service line?
  4. How does your product compare with others or your service with others (especially through the eyes of the customer)?

D. Reaction from specific prospective customers
  1. What prospective customers have you talked to?
  2. What was their reaction?
  3. Have they seen or tested a realistic prototype of the product or service?
  4. If so, what was their reaction?

E. Marketing activities
  1. What are your plans for
    a. Marketing strategy?
    b. Distribution?
    c. Promotion?
    d. Pricing?
    e. Sales appeals?
    f. Setting priorities among segments, applications, marketing activities?

F. Selling Activities
  1. How will you identify prospective customers?
  2. How will you decide which to contact and in what order?
  3. What level of selling effort will you have (for example, the number of salesmen)?
  4. What efficiency will you have (for example, how many calls per salesman)?

5. What conversion rates will you be able to obtain (for example, how many calls per demonstration; how many demonstrations per sale)?
6. How long will each of the above activities take in man-days? In elapsed time?
7. What will your order size be?
8. What evidence do you have to back up your answers to the estimates above?

This section on marketing analysis and marketing is often the most troublesome. Probably the most common single error is to assume you can validly predict what you can sell by gathering some general numbers on the size of the market, then project a market share for yourself. The argument goes like this: "We will be selling a semiautomatic typing machine. The total market for typewriters is about $600 million a year and growing 10 percent a year. Of this, 25 percent is automatic typewriters. Thus the portion available to us is $150 million the first year, $165 million the second year, $182 million the third, $200 million the fourth, and $220 million the fifth year. We project capturing $\frac{1}{2}$ of 1 percent the first year, or $750,000, and growing to 10 percent of the market, or $22 million, by the fifth year." Unless this kind of reasoning is backed up with favorable answers to the kinds of questions asked above, it is unconvincing and probably wrong.

V.   Technology
    A. What is the essence of your current technology?
    B. What is your patent or copyright position?
        1. How much is patented or copyrighted?
        2. How much can be patented or copyrighted?

3. How comprehensive and how effective will the patents or copyrights be?
4. Which companies have technology that is superior to yours?
5. Are there additional means of protecting your technology (such as secrecy, speed in putting out the product or service)?
6. How will your solution change during the next five years?

One common pitfall here is to compare the technology you are working on now and will have on the market in a year or two with that which competition has now. Instead, you should compare what you will have by the time you are in the market with what others will have *then*.

VI. Production/Operations
A. How will you accomplish production or conduct service operations?
1. How much will you do internally and by what methods?
2. How much through subcontracts?
B. What production or operating advantages do you have?
C. What is your present capacity for level of production or operations? How can this be expanded?

VII. Management and Ownership
A. Who are your key managers?
B. What are their skills and, particularly, their experience, and how does this relate to the success requirement of your venture?
C. What has their track record been, and how does this relate to your requirements?
D. What staff additions do you plan, when, and with what required qualifications?

E. Who is on your board of directors? What are the voting rules for your board?
F. Who are your stockholders, and how many shares does each own? (Include comments about options.)
G. What is the amount of stock authorized? Issued?

The most common problem here is failing to relate your team's capability to the success requirement of your business. In a proposal we saw recently the chief engineer was described as having a fine M.I.T. education and important-sounding job titles with sophisticated companies, but no mention was made of work he had actually done. This presentation left us wondering if he really could design the complex product he was supposedly going to design. (This one worked out well. It turned out under questioning that he had single-handedly designed about two-thirds of the existing competitive products and just come up with a still better way to do the job.)

Another frequent problem here is to find that the stock ownership is disproportionate to the contribution made. Investors, and sharp entrepreneurs as well, like to see the key contributors holding significant stock positions. This tends to ensure their continued contribution.

VIII. Funds Required and Their Uses
A. How much money do you require now?
B. How much will you require over the next five years, and when will it be required?
C. How will these funds be used?
D. What terms do you ask?

This section can probably be handled in the form of a simple prose presentation and need not include a formal sources and uses statement. Investors, of course, like to see money being used well and producing the kinds of results that will make the business successful. It makes them nervous to see entrepreneurs ask for money for high salaries, fancy offices, and so forth.

IX. Financial Data
    A. Present historical financial statements and projections for the next three to five years, including
      1. Profit-and-loss statements
      2. Balance sheets
      3. Cash budgets
    B. What key assumptions have been made in your pro formas, and how good are these assumptions?
X. Appendixes (as required)

Shortcuts and Pitfalls

This section describes various shortcuts and pitfalls to consider in writing your proposal.

Shortcuts

1. *Keep it short.* As mentioned earlier, 20 to 30 double-spaced typewritten pages should be enough to tell your story. If you need more, use it, but avoid lengthy explanations when a short one will do.

2. *Keep your priorities straight.* You have to cover only the key points in the proposal. Details can be included either in the backup material or as responses to questions. If you try to put in all the detail, you will have an unwieldy and probably unattractive proposal. (I saw one that was 348 pages.)

3. *Identify the tough questions first.* This advice will save you much

rewriting. Identify the tough questions first, and resolve as many as possible before you start writing. Often, halfway through writing, entrepreneurs find that a new question has arisen which will cause them to go back and rewrite what they have already done. Identifying such questions early saves time.

4. *Organize and outline.* Many proposals read like an entrepreneur's stream-of-consciousness, complete with redundancy and gaping holes. Organizing and outlining what you plan to say will not only prevent this but save you time as well.

5. *Use a sounding board.* Find someone who has had a lot of experience with start-up ventures, and talk over your venture with this person. It's almost impossible for one man or even a team of entrepreneurs to identify and resolve all the significant questions about a new venture.

Discussing it with an experienced, objective outsider will probably greatly improve your perspective and save you from falling into the more common traps. Although any of your advisors might serve as a sounding board, I think you are likely to get the most mileage out of a successful entrepreneur who is five to ten years ahead of you, a financial intermediary with lots of experience with start-ups, a management consultant specializing in small businesses, or a member of a venture capital group that is active in start-ups. In choosing a sounding board, make sure the person will give you the time you need.

Pitfalls

1. *Lack of evidence about your ability to sell.* This probably is the major pitfall. If it turned out to be only a *lack of evidence,* it wouldn't be so bad, but usually it turns out to be *lack of ability* to sell. For advice on how to market your product or service, see Chapter 11; for information on how to document this ability, see the earlier sections of this chapter.

2. *Trying to pursue too many opportunities.* One pollution control

product that we looked at seemed to have opportunities in 10 to 15 different industries, each requiring different channels of distribution. By trying to cover all these apparent opportunities, the entrepreneur with this product had his attention so badly diffused he wasn't accomplishing anything. The answer here was to pick the top two, focus on them, and ignore the rest for the time being. By doing this, the entrepreneur got moving and now has at least a beachhead.

3. *Not allowing enough time to raise the money.* You should probably allow at least 90 to 120 days from the time the proposal is completed in acceptable form. If you don't allow enough time, you run the risk not only of not getting your money when you need it but also of appearing so disorganized and desperate that you may not get it at all.

4. *Failing to ask for help when you need it.* Don't forget that your advisors are in the business of providing help and that your prospective investors are in the business of successfully investing money. These people want you to succeed. Often they can help you past trouble spots and want to do this. But first you have to let them know you need help.

In conclusion, it is worth your while to spend enough time on your financial proposal to make it a solid document. It is much better to confront difficult problems in your planning efforts than in the execution phase of your new venture.

7 SOURCES OF FINANCING
John J. Stuart, Jr.*

After you've prepared a comprehensive financial proposal, you're ready to tackle the problem that is probably the most unfamiliar to you—the actual search for money. As a healthy company matures, this function may be the day-to-day responsibility of a financial staff. But you haven't reached that point yet. In a new company the chances are good that all of the principals will find themselves more directly involved in raising money than they expected to be. Where do you begin? The variety of sources of financing for young firms is confusing. To understand which ones might be useful to you, you first need to understand the basic distinctions between the types of financing.

Types of Financing

Money is a commodity that can be obtained in three ways: you can buy it, you can lease it for a relatively long period, or you can rent it for a shorter time. In a nutshell, this is the distinction between equity financing, long-term financing, and short-term debt financing.

* John J. Stuart received his S.B. degree from the Sloan School of Management at M.I.T. He was a founder of Transyt Associates, Inc., and he is now president of the firm.

Equity Financing

Capital obtained in an equity transaction is permanently yours; that is, you don't have to pay it back. You have gained the right to use a specific amount of money in return for "a piece of the action," a share of the ownership of your company. Some form of equity financing is the type most commonly sought by new companies. Potential sources of equity financing for new enterprises include venture capital firms, investment bankers, Small Business Investment Corporations (SBICs), large corporations, occasionally pension funds or insurance companies, "angels," the public, friends and relatives, and, of course, yourself and your cofounders. Commercial banks and finance companies are not usually direct sources for equity financing, although they may provide helpful leads.

Long-Term Debt Financing

Some entrepreneurs are involved in businesses that require the purchase or long-term lease of valuable pieces of equipment and property. If these properties, or leaseholds, can be readily sold, it may be possible to obtain a portion of your early financing in the form of secured long-term debt. The first source to explore for such a financial arrangement is the person or company that is selling the property or equipment. He is more familiar with the value of the asset than anyone else, and he may be willing to carry a portion of the purchase price in the form of a long-term note. Some traditional financial institutions may also be interested in this type of financing.

Short-Term Debt Financing

Every entrepreneur hopes to get to the point where short-term debt financing is an integral part of his company's financial structure. For this you need sales. Without sales, a so-called short-term debt is more likely to be concealed equity, a gift from relatives, or a mortgage on your personal assets or on your

future earning power. Genuine short-term debt is character-
ized by self-liquidation: it is debt that is paid back out of
current cash flows within a specified period after that debt is
incurred (often 90 days). It is unlikely that you will have
enough sales at the beginning of your venture to qualify for any
substantial short-term debt financing. The traditional source
for short-term debt financing is the commercial bank. Another
source, one that is frequently overlooked by young companies,
is one or more of your suppliers who may be willing to extend
trade credit.

The Stages in a New Company's Development

Since most companies prefer equity financing in the start-up
phase, the remainder of the chapter will relate to sources for
this type of funding. The source that will fit your requirements
may change as your company develops. Even within the first
18 months of your company's existence, you will go through
several distinct stages of growth, and you may have to face the
problem of financing at each stage. To understand what is
meant by a "stage" of development, let's examine some
expressions frequently used in the business.

The Feasibility Stage
This first stage encompasses all the planning and development
activity that precedes the creation of a business entity. In this
stage, all the money raised is usually spent for market analyses
and surveys, patent searches and applications, legal consulta-
tions, technical feasibility analyses, and prototype product
development. The financing for these expenditures is frequently referred to as "front money" or "seed money."
Investors expect the entrepreneur to handle all or almost all of
the expenses of the feasibility stage himself. If this is not
possible, you will probably have to turn to private sources, such

as affluent individuals, rather than professional sources, such as venture capital firms. If times are good and you expect your company to be ready for a public stock offering at a very early date, you may be able to persuade some of the more speculative venture capital firms or investment bankers to invest in your company during the feasibility stage.

The Start-Up Stage

To investors, the term "start-up stage" does not necessarily refer to the same period of time as it does for entrepreneurs. As used by some financiers, the term refers to the period that begins with the creation of a business entity that is actively seeking sales and extends all the way to the break-even point. Most investors, however, consider a company to be out of the start-up stage when it reaches a particular sales volume, although this level may fall short of profitability. The idea here is that when you have reached a stage of marketing credibility —that is, when you have translated sales promise into sales reality you are no longer in the start-up stage. This point of marketing credibility varies according to the nature of the business. It may take two months or two years to get there. All the money you have raised to reach the end of the start-up stage is usually called "first-round financing" or "start-up capital." During the start-up stage, there will be more investment sources available to you than there were during the feasibility stage—but not a lot more. In addition to private individuals, you will find that some venture capital firms, SBICs, and large corporations occasionally invest in start-up companies.

It may be useful here to consider in more detail what is meant by a "round" of financing. You have undoubtedly heard statements like "It's hard to find first-round money" or "That venture capital company won't consider you until the second or third round." The "first round" is *not* the first sum of money raised by a new company, nor is the second sum of money the "second round," and so on. Expressions such as "first-round," "second-round," and "third-round" are used by investors to signify a company's development in terms of its sales and earnings—*not* in terms of its history of financing. Thus your first round of financing includes *all* the capital you raise to get your company to the end of the start-up stage, no matter how many separate financing deals this includes.

The Preprofitable Stage

If your company is not yet profitable but investors no longer consider you to be in a start-up phase, you will find yourself in a particularly ambiguous relationship with the money market. There is no commonly accepted term to describe this period. Additional financing during this time may be referred to as "first-round," "second-round," or even "round-and-a-half." If you have any significant profit potential, almost all equity sources will give you a courteous hearing during the preprofitable stage. But though you are no longer in a start-up position, you still cannot point to a bottom line that shows profit.

At least one successful entrepreneur thinks that the preprofitable stage is preferable to the growth stage when looking for big money. His reasoning is that the absence of a profit eliminates the possibility of using a simple criterion, such as earnings per share, to establish your company's value. Thus the potential investor has to do some spadework to find out if your deal is a good one, and that is precisely what you want him to do. This particular type of entrepreneur is in the minority, however. Although many financial analysts believe that there is too much emphasis on criteria such as price-earnings multiples, few would agree that lack of profit is an advantage in looking for money.

The Growth Stage

Once you have passed that magic milestone—profitability—and can show your potential for additional growth, you have clearly entered a new stage. Now you can negotiate with the financial community from a position of strength. If you still have difficulty in arranging the right kind of deal, however, give serious consideration to the kind of internal financing that you undoubtedly used during earlier stages. It is amazing how far the concerted belt-tightening of a determined group of principals and employees can carry a new enterprise. A case in point is an electro-optics company started by one entrepreneur from scratch in 1969. By 1971, the company had 18 professional employees, was showing profit, and was still growing. After only two years, it had annual sales approaching half a million dollars. This was achieved with a very limited infusion of equity financing from a few outside individuals, because the principals and employees systematically deferred large portions of their salaries to finance the growth of the company.

The Financial Climate

Discussions about sources of finance are liberally sprinkled with phrases such as "when times are good" and "when money is tight." Financial jargon is derived from the fact that money is a commodity and, like any other commodity, is subject to the law of supply and demand. At any point in time, there is a finite supply of money available for investment, and there is what sometimes seems like an infinite number of companies competing for that money. When the demand outstrips the supply by a very wide margin, the money market is "tight," and new ventures feel the pinch.

For example, the year 1970 saw a very tight market. So many large corporations were starved for cash to meet their obligations that the most conservative sources of financing, such as banks, could not meet the demand. The corporations then turned to other, more expensive sources, including some that historically have been considered sources of venture capital. High-quality growth-stage companies then found their sources of financing tied up elsewhere and had to turn to highly speculative sources. As a result, there were almost no sources left for companies in the feasibility and start-up stages; or, to use the jargon, "the front end was almost bone dry."

Contrast that period to the 1967–1968 money market. The public stock market was in a frenzy. Start-up companies were going public on a prayer and watching their stock prices jump overnight. This was called the "hot new issue" market. In that climate, many funding sources had to seek out new ways to put their money to work, and young companies could get a hearing from a wide variety of sources. This was one of the best times for new entrepreneurs.

What all this points to is that the availability of equity financing for a new company does not depend solely on the entrepreneur's ability to develop and sell his product. The financial climate and the supply of money available for the type of financing he needs may be crucial to the success of his enterprise. When the climate is good, the entrepreneur can be somewhat selective in his choice of sources to approach. When times are bad, he won't want to spend his time on any but the most likely prospects. To get a feel for the money market, the entrepreneur should become familiar with the financial sections of reliable newspapers and should talk to brokers, bankers, and other entrepreneurs.

Looking for a Source

As a new entrepreneur, your problem is how to find those sources that are most likely to be responsive to your company's needs. The first possibility that may occur to you is to send out copies of your business plan to several hundred potential sources of capital and then to wait. Before you do that, however, check the federal and state laws concerning the offering of securities. (See Capter 9.) Also consider the problem of overexposure. The term "shopping the deal" is used by many investors to describe this buckshot approach. They do not recommend it. One of the arguments against "shopping the deal" is the feedback loop that exists in the money market. Since different funding sources have different objectives, many of your inquiries will, of course, have negative results. Unfortunately, the fact of these rejections, but not the logic behind them, will become general knowledge in financial circles. It will then, perhaps, be more difficult for a favorably disposed source to buck the trend. Furthermore, "shopping the deal," in the eyes of most venture capitalists, is "unsophisticated." It proves that the entrepreneur does not understand the subtleties of the money market—that the "right" source will enhance his marketing credibility, will help with planning, and will remain available for future financial negotiations.

Venture capitalists like to say that you should pick your money source as carefully as you would a marriage partner. During the feasibility and start-up stages of your new enterprise, you will probably be unable to follow this advice. Finding any source sometimes seems impossible.

Three examples may shed some light on how little of the fund-raising process is mysterious and how much is hustle, strategy, and whom you are lucky enough to know or contact. In the first case, two hardworking and conscientious entrepreneurs decided that they had developed some insight into a particular technology around which they wanted to form a company. They first spent their own money to open an office, to build prototypes of their equipment, and to build a record of being in business even though no sales were made. After exhausting their personal funds ($15,000), they set out to find "venture capital." In a period of less than five minutes they were able to contact all their friends who had enough personal funds to finance their next stage of development. One friend did agree to come on their board of directors and to help them look for funds. He set up meetings with a number of major corporations and venture capital firms. All of these companies gave the new entrepreneurs a polite hearing and advised them to look elsewhere. Then out of the blue an old classmate who had heard of their search for investors said he would be willing to act as an intermediary for several wealthy acquaintances who might be interested in the company. These contacts ultimately made a substantial investment—$150,000. The moral of this story is that while you do not want to "shop your deal around" to too many firms or individuals, you should make it widely known that you are looking for funds so that those who believe in you can help you.

My second example involves corporate participation. Again we have two entrepreneurs. Both were about forty and had pursued successful business careers. One had even had profit-and-loss responsibility for a division of a sophisticated consulting company. As a result of a change in the business direction of this company, they decided to go out on their own. When they made their decision known, a large firm, one of their previous clients, asked them to form a company and to continue their development of an earlier project. This large corporation felt that the new system would benefit them and could also be sold to others to become the basis of a very profitable business. The situation in which the corporation is a customer as well as an investor is probably one of the few in which corporations are today making venture investments.

In rare instances the public may also turn out to be available for venture capital. A few years ago a consulting company was formed by going immediately to the public. In this case ten entrepreneurs with consulting and academic backgrounds felt that if they pooled all the people they knew, they could sell enough stock among them to finance their company. The ten formed a corporation and filed for an intrastate offering. Under the laws of the state each of the founders of the company was able to sell stock to the public, provided the sale was based on the state-approved offering circular the founders had prepared with the aid of their attorneys. After six months of selling stock they were able to raise about $200,000. With this money five of the ten founders went to work full time, and the others assisted the company in a consulting capacity. Where an underwriter is not used, as in this case, it will usually take a lot of founders to be able to develop the necessary stock distribution. The real advantage of going to the public is that very often you do not have to give up as much equity as is required in private offerings.

A brief description makes the process seem easy. But in the first case there were countless telephone calls and many fruitless meetings with potential investors. Nine months passed from the preparation of the business plan until the receipt of the check. The second example was considerably different since the corporation was the only source of capital contacted. However, a complete business plan and extensive negotiations were required to complete the transaction. Finally, the selling of stock to the public required an interminable number of presentations. These repetitive presentations were enough to tax any Broadway actor's reserve of spontaneity.

Individual Sources of Financing

In the early stages of your development, individual or private sources are more likely to be attracted to your enterprise than professional sources. (For the purposes of this discussion, I have defined a single decision maker who invests his own money as

an "individual" source and all other sources as "professional.")
When an individual does not have to justify his financial
decisions to anyone else, noneconomic criteria are sometimes as
important as economic criteria. This can be important to the
entrepreneur whose venture is still in the feasibility stage. For
example, an aerospace engineer, distressed by the effects of the
industry's decline on his career potential, may be looking for
an investment opportunity that could lead to a new career.
Someone facing mandatory retirement may be looking for a
new enterprise in which to invest his time and money. A
successful senior executive may enjoy the challenge of helping
a small new company get off the ground, giving it the benefit of
his contacts and experience as well as capital. Some investors
are interested in companies that will improve the environment.
Some would like to indulge a long-standing avocation. The
possibilities are endless and impossible to predict. The entrepreneur who seeks an individual source should try to take
advantage of noneconomic factors if and when they enter the
picture.

There are several types of individuals who may become
sources of financing: the principals themselves, relatives and
friends, professional associates and advisors, wealthy individual
investors, and the public at large.

The Principals

The founders of your company will probably be its major
source of financing during the feasibility stage. In dollars and
cents this probably means a bare minimum of several thousand
dollars in out-of-pocket expenses. Moreover, you will probably
have to survive for some time on substantially reduced salaries.
In one case where the stakes were enormous, two entrepreneurs
sustained their company's feasibility and marketing stage for
21 months, each working full time without any salary. Neither
of them was wealthy, but both were willing to commit
everything they had to their venture. It usually makes good

sense to assume that you and your partners will have to live for at least six to 12 months on half your normal salaries. This assumption may not be included in your formal business plan but should be part of your personal plan.

Relatives and Friends
There is no denying that mixing business with family affairs is risky. There is also no denying that relatives are among the most likely sources for personal financial help, if not for outright investment in your company. Since your request for financial help will probably be given more weight than an investment proposition from a stranger, you will have to evaluate your own hopes and expectations for your company. Obviously, you would not ask relatives to finance a venture that had dubious chances for success. But do not let pride create an artificial barrier. If you believe in your enterprise and have relatives who are in a position to provide help, give them the opportunity to do something they may really want to do. Friends, too, may be difficult to approach, although you may be able to discuss the venture somewhat more objectively with them than with relatives. If you are reluctant to approach friends, you may be protecting them from making what you yourself feel would be a bad investment. Study your own motives, and trust your friends' ability to make intelligent decisions.

Professional Advisors and Associates
Perhaps you have already asked your lawyer to exchange legal services for equity in your company. As discussed in Chapter 9, some attorneys question the propriety of such investments. Nevertheless, many small companies still finance their early legal expenses in this manner. You may also be able to interest your accountant, your directors, and your key employees to invest in your enterprise.

Recently the principals of a new company financed its

feasibility stage on their own and then raised start-up capital by seeking investors who had something to offer the company in the way of technical or marketing skills. These investors all became cofounders of the corporation. They served as directors, made marketing contacts, assisted in the production of mock-ups, performed design analyses, and supported a wide range of business activities on a part-time basis. They all had responsible full-time jobs elsewhere but were, in effect, part-time principals rather than outside investors. The only full-time principals were the original founders. How much money can be raised in this way? In the case above, the amount was about $60,000. In a few similar cases, between $25,000 and $50,000 was raised from ten to 15 part-time associates. The same amount might be raised from relatives and friends, but the potential impact of the investment is much more powerful when the investors become actively involved insiders. If you decide to try this approach, it will probably take three to four months of tough negotiations to create a working team.

Affluent Individuals
If your minimum start-up requirements exceed $50,000–75,000 you may have to search out a few affluent individuals who "dabble" in speculative investments. They do exist, but despite what you may have heard, they are hard to find. Sometimes it is possible to put together a $100,000–200,000 package by tracking down about a dozen doctors, lawyers, executives, and other professional people and forming, in effect, a syndicate. When money is tight, however, this type of opportunity is one of the first to vanish. Your best approach to affluent investors is through friends, acquaintances, and business and professional associates who can help you establish some degree of personal credibility. It may take a chain of two or three personal contacts to reach each potential investor. Don't overlook the people who handle your financial, personal, business, and legal

affairs. Your broker, banker, lawyer, accountant, realtor, and insurance agent may help you make contact with individual sources. Eventually, however, you may have to turn to a "finder."

A finder is a professional source of contacts, but he does not take an active role in negotiations once he has helped you contact a prospective investor. If a finder leads you to someone who invests in your venture within some reasonable period of time, he is entitled to a fee, usually a percentage of the amount of money raised through his contacts. You should reach an agreement about fees before he actively starts working for you. Most agreements between an entrepreneur and a finder include a statement that the finder is an independent contractor, not your employee, thus avoiding any liability to you as a result of his actions. In addition, an agreement usually specifies the degree and duration of exclusivity that the finder will enjoy. It is reasonable for him to ask for an exclusive arrangement for a limited time for specific contacts with whom he has a particularly good working relationship. But it is not in your best interests to give a finder a blanket exclusive for an unlimited time. If he is unsuccessful, you want to be free to reopen discussions through other channels with the sources he has contacted on your behalf. Finally, there is the fee itself. You need to stipulate whether it is to be paid in cash, securities, or some combination thereof. You should also make it clear that he doesn't get his money until you get yours. The amount is subject to negotiation. A formula that is sometimes used is called "the 5-4-3-2-1 principle." The finder receives 5 percent of the first million dollars raised, 4 percent of the second million, 3 percent of the third million, 2 percent of the fourth million, 1 percent of any excess over $4 million up to $25 million, and 0.5 percent of any excess over $25 million. For smaller deals, a finder's fee may be 6 percent or higher. If a finder suggests an agreement that goes significantly beyond these benchmarks, don't hesitate to ask why. How do you find a finder? The same way you are trying to find investors—through contacts. You will probably discover that, once the word gets around that you are looking, a finder will find you.

The affluent individual investor whom you contact on your own or with the help of a finder is not in the same category as friends, relatives, or ordinary professional and business associates. For one thing, he has a wider range of opportunities for investment. Your friends and relatives may look upon your company as their once-in-a-lifetime opportunity. You don't have that going for you in negotiations with the wealthy investor. He will feel no pressure to invest in your company today, because he knows that he will get a chance at another promising opportunity tomorrow. Furthermore, if his wealth has been recently acquired through his own hard work, he may demand a lot more for his money than you feel is reasonable. In the realm of business folklore, doctors have a reputation for driving such hard bargains that they kill the motivation of the entrepreneur (and ultimately doom the enterprise). At the other end of the spectrum, some entrepreneurs claim that individuals whose wealth is second- or third-generation take a more relaxed attitude when negotiating terms. Your own experience may not bear out these generalizations, but they are widespread enough to merit consideration.

All wealthy individuals are concerned about taxes. Take the time to put together a sales talk that will show a high-bracket investor how he can use your venture as a tax shelter. Study the laws about "Subchapter S" corporations and "Section 1244" stock (Chapter 9), intercorporation contracts that convert part of the investment into expenses, and any other strategies you and your professional advisors can devise.

The Public

A public offering is in the same category as other individual sources of equity financing if you sell directly to the public yourself. For stock worth $500,000 or more, you will need the services of a professional underwriter, an investment banker. But for a smaller amount, you can "blue-sky"—that is, go public on your own. This means making fewer concessions than with other sources of equity financing, but it also has drawbacks. You and your coprincipals, your associates, and your employees will have to make innumerable contacts and public presentations for several months. To comply with federal and state securities regulations, you will need to spend more front (that is, your own) money than otherwise. Furthermore, professional equity sources would much prefer to get involved with you before you make a public offering, so you should be fairly certain that this approach will raise enough money to take you to the point where additional financing will be no problem. Many entrepreneurs consider a blue-sky public offering only as a last resort. But with the right combination of salesmanship, stamina, and luck, some entrepreneurs have been able to raise several hundred thousand dollars.

Professional Sources of Financing

Unlike individual sources of financing, each investment decision from a professional source is made by several people. Convincing one member of a professional group is just the first step, and investment decisions are likely to be made strictly on the basis of business criteria. In addition to basic numbers, one factor that is very important in dealings with professional sources is your track record. The question becomes: What have you done in the past? It is a dressed-up version of personal credibility. Your friends and relatives and your close business and professional associates know that you are honest, smart, and hardworking. But the usual professional source doesn't know a thing about you. He wants concrete evidence of your performance potential in a business environment—what is known in the jargon as "P & L," profit-and-loss responsibility.

For inexperienced entrepreneurs, this will pose a problem and is a good reason to choose associates who have had entrepreneurial experience.

Venture Capital Firms

These are middlemen for dealing with speculative sources. Sometimes they have direct management responsibility for the investment of their source's funds; sometimes they simply act as a go-between. For example, some venture capital firms manage the speculative investments of one wealthy family, or a coalition of private individuals, or a corporation. Others are independent and deal with a broader field of investors. Independent firms may rely totally on informal relationships developed through their business associations and activities. The venture capital firm's relationship with sources of money involves much more responsibility than does that of the individual middleman or finder. The firm takes an active role in the decision-making process and, from the entrepreneur's point of view, may be indistinguishable from the source. Occasionally, a venture capital firm may play an extremely active role in rounding out an entrepreneur's package. If members of the firm believe your deal has merit but lacks something essential, they may try to help you find the missing ingredient, such as a key executive or a related product line. Involvement to this extent is unusual but not unknown.

If the venture capital firm is not formally related to a specific source, it will make its profit in the same way as the finder: by charging a percentage of the final investment. The fee may be in the same range as the finder's fee discussed earlier, at least in terms of percentages. Then why deal at all with individual finders rather than independent venture capital firms? When the money market is healthy, you may have an option. When money is tight, however, venture capital firms may be looking for deals with less risk than your new enterprise involves.

Investment Banking Firms

These firms are also middlemen, but they provide much broader contacts than even an independent venture capital firm. They can provide the same kind of service as the venture capital firm; that is, they may act as agents by taking your package to other investors. They also have direct control over large amounts of money and because of this can act as underwriters. An underwriter insures or guarantees that you will receive a certain amount of money from a specific financing package, such as the sale of company stock. In essence, the underwriter buys the package at a negotiated price and then resells it at a higher price. If there is a large amount of money involved, underwriters usually band together in a syndicate to spread the risk of the offering. The underwriting function of investment bankers is not likely to be of immediate concern to you as a new entrepreneur. With some exceptions, most investment banks consider it too risky to underwrite financing packages for new companies. Even with a "hot new issue" market, many established investment banking firms will not handle an underwriting for a start-up company. This doesn't mean that investment bankers are always unwilling to help a new entrepreneur. By virtue of their wide range of investment activity, they have a large number of contacts in the financial community. If you can convince a well-known investment banker to recommend your package, this will carry great weight with prospective sources. Since you will be needing an investment banker some day, you should begin to talk to one early in your development. But be realistic about the immediate possibilities.

Small Business Investment Corporations (SBICs)

These are special investment corporations chartered by the federal government, to stimulate the formation and growth of small businesses. SBICs get tax breaks in return for taking higher-risk investment positions than some sources are willing to accept. They must comply with regulations governing the size of companies they invest in and the amount of equity they take. Nothing in the law says that SBICs must finance every new venture, however. They tend to favor new companies started by people with extensive management experience who are buying into existing markets. In effect, SBICs are no more or less likely to invest in your venture than any other professional source.

Large Corporations
In the 1960s, it was fashionable to talk about the role of big corporations as a source of venture capital. Several corporations organized and funded specific venture capital activities. Others talked about the need to spin off new enterprises to avoid losing the entrepreneurial talent that was constantly emerging within their organizations. But a funny thing happened on the way through the cash crunch of 1970. Many corporations had to scramble just to handle their own cash-flow problems. Their venture capital investments took a back seat. Nevertheless, there are still some big corporations that are formally involved in venture capital activity. When they evaluate your deal, they will usually want to know how well your business fits in with their own interests. If you have something that relates particularly well to their business, you may stand a chance of receiving their help even if they aren't officially involved in venture capital activity.

If the corporation you are considering does not have a venture capital office or subsidiary, look for its office of mergers and acquisitions or the office of corporate development. Explore the possibility of getting marketing help from them, of forming a joint venture, or of being awarded a small contract to help them become your supplier or vice versa. In other words, try to convince them that your success is in their best interests. If they accept this assessment, chances are good that your financing problems will be solved. Many corporations, however, resist entanglements with small outside entities. And even if you are able to convince them to help you, it will take a long time to complete negotiations. If you need to get your company rolling, it is not realistic to plan on a big corporation as a near-term source for your start-up financing.

Other Sources
You may have heard that large institutions, such as insurance companies and pension funds, are sources of equity financing for new ventures. In the broadest sense this is true. But such sources are usually interested in ventures such as a new skyscraper or a land development project. They do invest in the start-up of new companies, but they favor proved management teams buying into traditional markets. If you have a good contact with a source in this category, try your luck. Otherwise, don't waste too much valuable time.

A Possible Strategy

Decide whether you can survive for at least one year at half your present salary or less. Take a hard look at your business plan; pick a sales milestone that will take three to six months to achieve with an outside equity investment of no more than $25,000–50,000 in cash. Start probing for interest from friends, relatives, and potential business associates (after consulting your attorney). Contact some finders. As soon as you get enough positive feedback to suggest that you can successfully assemble a deal, take your package to a few select professional sources. Choose sources that have something "extra" to offer (for example, corporations in your business area, investment banks that have underwritten public offerings for similar ventures), or sources with whom you have good personal contacts, or sources that are geographically accessible. Tell them what you are doing, that you don't expect them to get involved right away, but that you will need financing when you reach that first sales milestone. Unless they twist your arm to take their money immediately, continue putting together a deal with individual sources. Keep the professional sources informed of your progress. If you get your money from modest sources, continue talking to finders. And continue to communicate with professional sources once you are under way. If you haven't begun serious negotiations with a source within three or four months, start planning to blue-sky a public placement. Then work night and day to meet that sales milestone!

What are the advantages to this strategy? It is under your own control. In particularly good times, it can't hurt you, and it may make you stand out among new ventures. In bad times, it will at least help you get off the ground.

8 FINANCIAL DEALS FOR PRIVATE FUNDS

Daniel J. Holland *

While the relative importance of the deal consideration in the overall entrepreneurial activity is difficult to determine, it can be said for certain that the first deal will be only one of many, regardless of success or trouble in the future. In the perfect situation, the entrepreneurs through good planning and forecasting determine their short- and long-term needs and identify financial sources whose expectations are consistent with their own. Under these conditions, the terms of the deal are easily negotiated, the company meets its plan, and all prosper and live happily ever after. Unfortunately, no examples of such a perfect situation seem to exist. Any activity of this nature is affected by a combination of variables and is subject to continual change and modification. When success is achieved, and fortunately it is achieved often, it is usually in a form not originally contemplated. Consequently, continual revision of the original plan usually occurs, requiring negotiation and compromise between the entrepreneurs and the sources of funds. General Georges F. Doriot, president of American Research and Development Corporation, has stated

* Daniel J. Holland received his S.B. degree in mechanical engineering from M.I.T. and his M.B.A. from the Harvard Business School. In 1969 he joined American Research and Development Corporation, one of the early and most prestigious of the venture capital firms. He is currently a vice-president of American Research and Development, now a division of Textron Corporation.

that there are only two times to raise equity for a new company. The first time is on the basis of hopes and dreams and the next time on the basis of profits and growth. Merchandising or selling hopes and dreams is really what the entrepreneur is doing with the development of a business plan, selection of teammates and partners, and so forth. These plans, proposals, product prototypes, and other concrete items help to give substance to the hopes and dreams and provide a basis for initial negotiations. However, modifications, compromise, and renegotiation of the initial deal are more easily accomplished if the hopes and dreams are understood and accepted at the outset.

Before seeking investors and negotiating deals, it is imperative for the entrepreneurs to maximize the value of the strengths they bring to the bargaining table. A well-defined, easily read, thoughtful, and concise business plan with appropriate backup information is an absolute minimum. A patented (or patentable) product or proprietary process is helpful in setting relative values, and a working prototype is superior to drawings and concepts. A team of people committed through the investment of time and personal savings is of much more value than a collection of résumés of outstanding people who will be available if money is found. A previously investigated and easily verifiable market need and the method for reaching this market can attach great value to the proposed new business. These and other items in the planning process are important in "selling" investors and in determining the value of the entrepreneurs relative to the value of the dollars and other contributions of the investors. More important, such considerations are essential to the eventual success of the business.

Determination of Initial Value

For our point of departure, we will first consider a straight equity investment in which a certain portion of the common stock is sold to the investors and the rest retained by the entrepreneurs. The advantages are obvious. If the entrepreneurs retain greater than 50 percent ownership, they control the company. An equity investment does not have interest payment requirements, and the company can show a profit sooner because of this. Also, it is simple, clean, and uncomplicated. The disadvantages of limiting consideration only to equity are very real but not as obvious. Many sources of funds prefer to invest on a debt or preferred stock basis. Eliminating these sources from consideration reduces the market for investment funds. Theoretically, more equity must be sold to investors since this carries a higher risk than other forms of investment. Never a substitute, but always helpful, is the ability of the source to attract other investors, either new or in the future. Some firms or individuals are considered "lead investors," usually because of a reputation gained from successful investments. They can be very helpful in bringing in other investors, whether at the outset or when additional funds are required. "Staying power," the ability and willingness to wait a long time if necessary to obtain a return on the investment, is another important characteristic to look for in an investor. Everyone hopes for a quick return, but be wary of those sources that *demand* a quick return. Often a good feel for this can be obtained by learning the history of other investments made by the potential source. This is a difficult characteristic to determine, but one that can greatly affect the conduct and future of the venture.

The amount of equity that must be sold to an investor is a function of the bargaining strengths and selling capabilities of the investors and the entrepreneurs as well as a function of economic conditions and the supply of investment dollars. In some cases, as much as 50 to 80 percent of the initial equity has been sold to the investors at the time of start-up. In fact, Digital Equipment Corporation of Maynard, Massachusetts, one of the great success stories in American industry, sold 70 percent of its equity to American Research and Development Corporation in 1957. This amount of ownership can often be obtained by strong investors who put up all of the initial money and who possess many of the bargaining strengths or characteristics discussed above. In order for the entrepreneurs to retain a greater proportion of ownership, they must either invest their own money on the same basis as the investors or convince the investors that they are contributing dollar equivalent factors to the venture such as patents, skills, and experience not obtainable elsewhere. Naturally, if there is concern about the capabilities and long-term views of the investors, then the entrepreneurs should do everything possible to sell less than 50 percent of the equity and thereby retain voting control.

At the other end of the spectrum, it is sometimes possible to sell as little as 10 percent of the company for the initial funds. This usually requires a variety of favorable circumstances: intense competition among investors looking for new opportunities; a reasonable expectation of short-term profits; a well-protected product or process, with little development required and good profit margins; an impressive team of entrepreneurs. One danger in this approach is that additional funds may be required in the future under less favorable circumstances, and the high price paid by the original investors will not be obtainable. For example, suppose an initial investment of $300,000 is made for 10,000 shares of stock at $30 a share. An additional 90,000 shares are retained by the entrepreneur. This "values" the company initially at $3 million (100,000 shares at $30). Let's suppose that the company makes good but needs an additional $500,000. The company finds new investors but they are willing to "value" the company at only $1 million. They want 50 percent of the equity, 10,000 shares at $5 a share. Obviously, the original investors are going to be unhappy and even unfriendly under these circumstances. Their investment is now worth only one-sixth of its original cost, even though the company has made progress. The entrepreneur, with his 90,000 shares out of 200,000, now owns only 45 percent of the company. He no longer has voting control.

Sometimes the original investors demand preemptive rights—that is, the right to maintain their original percentage of ownership during any subsequent private placements. This complicates future fund raising for the entrepreneur, especially when new capital is offered at a price below the cost of the original investment. In the above example, preemptive rights would entitle the original investors to 20,000 shares at $5 a share. The entrepreneur would now have only 30 percent ownership in his company.

Utilization of Future Progress to Modify Initial Value

Determining the initial "value" of a company is extremely difficult. Investors usually want a return of several times their investment over a reasonable period. The entrepreneur naturally wants a significant degree of ownership in the company he has built. Consequently, there are many different types of agreements negotiated between entrepreneurs and investors which attempt to recognize the initial inexactness of valuation by establishing values based on future performance criteria. For example, an initial, but insufficient, investment may be made at a low price, with future investment committed at higher prices if and when the company meets certain goals of product development, sales, profits, and so forth. There are several drawbacks to this plan. If the entrepreneur does not meet his goals, a difficult renegotiation of terms is necessary. On the other hand, sometimes the entrepreneur meets his goals only to find that the investors do not have the funds to meet their obligation.

There are other ways to overcome the initial difficulties of valuation. The entrepreneur may be given the right to buy out part or all of the original investment at some time in the future at a price that reflects the rate of return expected by the investor. As an example, suppose that the investors buy 30,000 shares of stock for $300,000 ($10 a share) and the entrepreneurs retain 10,000, or 25 percent, of the company, with three-year options on 20,000 of the investors' shares, at $40 a share. This would be a return on the investment of four times the cost of the investors' shares. The entrepreneur has the chance to regain 75 percent ownership in his company, and the investors still have a stake in the company's future. To exercise his options, the entrepreneur would need to find $800,000. Presumably he would borrow against the value of the stock he owns (and will own) in the company. It is difficult, but not impossible, to find investors who are willing to limit their gain to a specific rate of return. And it could also be difficult, but again not impossible, for the entrepreneur to find the funds necessary to exercise his option.

There are variations to this plan. An entrepreneur may negotiate options or warrants that will enable him to purchase a certain percentage of the company at a favorable price at some future date. Using the example given above, let us suppose that the entrepreneur negotiates an option to buy 20,000 shares of the company's stock at some future date, at a price higher than the original investment price of $10 a share, but less than four times the return price of $40 a share—say, $25 a share. If the entrepreneur could raise $500,000, he would then own 30,000 shares. In order to borrow this kind of money, using his stock as collateral, the stock would have to have a value of at least $100 a share, preferably with a public market for the stock. Under these conditions, the original investors would be very happy with their $10 stock.

Occasionally an investor, such as an industrial corporation, wants to be able to control or to own the company completely at some time in the future. One method of accomplishing this is sometimes called the "double trigger" option. Party A (either the investor or the entrepreneur) offers to buy Party B's interests at a certain price; Party B then has a certain amount of time to buy Party A's interests at the price offered by A, or to sell to A at that price. In other words, either party can buy out the other at a price determined by the first party to make an offer.

Some investors, and most entrepreneurs, are willing to negotiate performance incentives when structuring an investment. The main objective is to return some of the equity to the entrepreneurs as various goals are met. When the goals are reached, the value of the company—and thereby the value of the investment—is increased. For instance, the entrepreneur's warrant or option prices, discussed above, could be tied to some low multiple of earnings per share, whereas the actual value of the company would be at some much higher multiple. Using the same example, let us assume that the entrepreneur has warrants to buy stock at five times the earnings per share (eps), and suppose that the company operates in an industry that typically values such stock at 20 times eps and, in addition, that the company projects earnings of $120,000 in the year when the option may be exercised. Thus the eps would be $2 a share on 60,000 shares (the original 40,000 plus the 20,000 warrants), and the entrepreneurs would buy these at five times $2 ($10 a share), for a total of $200,000. At a multiple of 20 times one, the investors' stock would be worth $40 per share or four times their initial investment—in line with the anticipated rate of return.

Performance incentives are very popular with confident, aggressive entrepreneurs but difficult to sell to many investors. Negotiations may become bogged down in issues conducive to the proper start and operation of the business. The result may be complex legal documents and reporting controls that are

burdensome, irritating, and perhaps even obsolete as the
nature of the business changes. Incentives, to be meaningful
and measurable, must be specific. It is difficult to take into
account the many factors that could actually help the company in the future but adversely affect the incentives. Con-
versely, some factors might help the company meet the
incentives while actually inhibiting company growth. In either
case, the incentives turn into constraints. For example, when
profits are used to determine performance, there may be a
complete absence of product development expenditures or a
delay in establishing a sales force. While such actions may
enhance short-term profits, they could drastically undermine
the long-term success of the company.

Under some circumstances, the company can be structured
with two classes of stock, one class for the entrepreneur and one
for the investors, with the investors' stock carrying preferential
rights for payment in the event of liquidation. This can limit
the "downside" risk for the investor, especially if the initial
investment is used for assets that would have some value in the
event of liquidation, such as standard machinery and equipment, land, and buildings. The two classes of stock may carry
different voting rights. Generally, the entrepreneur's stock will
control the company, elect a majority of the directors, and so
forth, as long as the company proceeds in a positive direction.
However, it is also usual for the investors to make some
provision for gaining control if the company runs into trouble
and deteriorates to a point where the investment is in jeopardy.
These provisions usually center around financial measure-
ments, such as nonpayment of dividends, operating losses, and
decreases in net worth or working capital. From the entrepreneur's viewpoint, such arrangements sometimes seem advantageous since he retains control of the company as long as
progress is being made and sells less equity than in a straight
stock deal because the investors' risk is, theoretically, less. In

addition to losing control of the company under certain circumstances, the main disadvantages to such arrangements are the complications that arise during future financial negotiations, especially with other private funds. If such negotiations are conducted while the company is in trouble, the new investors will not want their investment to be subordinate to that of the original investors. The original investors, in turn, will be unwilling to relinquish their liquidation position if it has any value. One variation of this arrangement is to issue only one class of stock, with a "side" agreement between the original investors and the entrepreneurs that gives the investors rights to any funds received in liquidation up to the amount of their investment, with any excess going to the entrepreneurs.

Use of Debt/Equity Investments

So far, we've discussed only investments dealing with stock. However, many private funds prefer to use a debt vehicle with equity consideration for their investments and, on occasion, some combination of debt and equity. We will consider three different forms: (1) a combination of debt and equity; (2) convertible debt; and (3) debt with warrants.

The first case—a combination of debt and equity—is relatively simple. Part of the investment is made in stock, and the rest is loaned to the company at a negotiated interest rate, with payment terms determined by the financial projections. Theoretically, the investor will require less equity under these conditions (as opposed to a complete stock transaction) since the debt part of the investment does not have as much risk as the stock part.

Basically, convertible debt is a loan that carries negotiated interest and payment terms and can be "converted" into stock at some future date. This is probably one of the most popular investment vehicles for most private funds. Typically, repayment is not required for several years since the investor usually desires a comfortable period of time to evaluate the company's progress before making the decision on whether to convert to stock. The entrepreneur would be wise to begin repayment of this loan within a reasonable period of time (perhaps two to four years) and to base rate of repayment on the company's ability to pay, as indicated by cash flow projections. Occasionally, the conversion terms are such that the stock conversion price in the early years is less than that in the later years, reflecting the company's anticipated increase in value as it grows. Usually, the investor has the right to convert the loan to stock at any time, but can be forced to do so only when loan payments are due.

The third general form of debt investment is a loan with warrants enabling the investor to purchase stock at some future time. Under these conditions, debt repayment can begin sooner than with a convertible loan since the life of the warrants is usually independent of the terms of the debt. Otherwise, this form of investment is similar in most respects to a convertible loan.

Restrictions of Debt Investments

Common to all of the preceding methods is the use of debt as a vehicle for investment. Many reasons are given by investors for preferring this method. First of all, it limits their risk, relative to the entrepreneur's, in the event of sale or liquidation of the venture. Second, the interest payments provide some return or operating income for the investor and are tax-deductible by the company. Third, it provides a means for the debt holders to gain control of the company if management gets into trouble.

Many things can happen when a company runs into difficulties. An investor has several options. Obviously, one option is to do nothing and simply hope the company can solve its problems without help or pressure. If the investors have voting control, they can replace management, sell or merge the company, dissolve the company and sell the assets, and so forth. If the investors have a debt instrument that is in default, they can usually demand payment—which the company is probably unable to meet. Under extreme circumstances the investors can use the threat of "calling the loan" and forcing the company into bankruptcy to gain concessions or action from the owners/managers. These negotiations can lead to many different conditions, such as increased equity for the investors and perhaps ultimate voting control of the stock.

The advantage to the entrepreneur in attracting debt investment is they that he can sell less ownership in his company since less risk for the investor is involved in a debt investment than in a stock investment. Typically, this debt is legally subordinate to certain other loans and is thus considered as effective equity by banks or other lenders when they are considering a loan to the company. Debt-related investments are especially appropriate to those ventures where profits and cash flow are expected relatively soon and with a high degree of probability. Only then can the terms of the debt be met. If the terms are not met, the debt holders can gain control of the company. Some or all of the following terms, provisions, or default conditions might be included in a debt instrument:

1. A repayment schedule is usually designed to fit the cash flow projections. Funds to meet these payments are derived from profits or from raising other funds in the future. Failure to meet these payments can mean renegotiation of the terms of the investment and/or control of the company by the noteholder.

2. Interest rates usually reflect current bank lending rates; interest is usually payable at least annually or semiannually.

3. Future borrowings are usually limited to borrowings from commercial banks, and the company is prohibited from pledging assets to secure loans.

4. Minimum limits are set on such balance sheet items as

working capital and net worth. If these items go below these limits, the loan is considered to be in default.

5. The sale or merger of the company or the purchase of another company usually requires consent of the noteholders.

6. A variety of other limitations or provisions can also be included, such as maximum salaries for officers, limitations on profit-sharing and pension plans and other types of deferred compensations, and no redemption of stock by the company.

It should be kept in mind that the purpose of such provisions is to protect the investors in the event of deterioration or catastrophe in the company. If a good working relationship exists between the entrepreneurs and investors, it is not usually necessary for the investors to use these provisions to protect their investment. Whenever any provision adversely affects the proper conduct of the company, it is rarely difficult to obtain a waiver from the noteholder, providing a good relationship exists. It should be apparent to the entrepreneur that it is necessary to understand the various provisions and, more important, the reasoning behind each provision before signing the note. Also, it should be very obvious that such deals are best made with investors of good reputation, with a history of successful deals of this type and, of course, long-term views consistent with those of the entrepreneur.

Other Investment Terms and Provisions

Clearly, the number and types of provisions that can be included in debt instruments, and occasionally in stock restriction agreements, are limited only by the imagination and experience of the investors and entrepreneurs, though occasionally there are legal constraints. For instance, investors may require an agreement giving them such things as (1) preemptive rights (the right to invest in any future sale of stock on a pro rata basis); (2) piggyback provisions (the right to sell some or all of their stock in the company whenever the company sells stock to the public); (3) forced registration, whereby the company will, at its expense, register and sell the investors' stock to the public whenever the investor requests such an action. These and other restrictions and legal provisions are explained more fully in Chapter 9.

Many investors are fearful of becoming locked into a mediocre company that might not have the need or ability to go public. If the investors do not have voting control or some form of debt instrument, there is no way for them to get their money out. Consequently, they may require some means for converting their stock into a loan at some point in the future. This form of provision is rarely used, however, since most investors prefer a convertible loan.

Nonfinancial Considerations

At this point it is worthwhile to consider the values or contributions other than dollars which investors can bring to the negotiating table and ultimately apply to the success of the venture. It is rare indeed for an investor to invest money and then leave the venture alone. Other possible contributions are very important in determining the value of the investor to the entrepreneur and, subsequently, the degree of equity participation. We will attempt to define some of the more important characteristics of various investors.

The most important characteristic of an investor is the size of his investment relative to the resources he is willing to commit to the new venture (rather than relative to his total resources). As stated earlier, the first deal is one of many, and subsequent funds might be required from the original investor. This is especially true if the venture encounters unanticipated problems or if the economic climate is such that other funds are difficult to find. In this regard, the investors' long-term views about the venture are especially important. If the source has invested in other ventures, this experience should be discussed openly. If this is a new endeavor for the source, then their long-term views are especially important. It is usually very difficult to get written commitments for future investments, and thus it is important to have a good feeling for the investors' attitudes.

There are a variety of other investor characteristics that are also important. For instance, some investors can supply temporary personnel, such as a controller to help set cost standards, a technical expert to help solve a nonrecurring technical problem, a real estate expert to help with the initial decisions in this area, and so on. This is especially true of the venture capital operations of industrial companies or other large organizations such as banks and insurance companies that can call on their operating staff to assist the new venture. In some instances, investors will have such people directly on their staff and are therefore easily identified. Often, however, they too must seek this help elsewhere, perhaps from the staffs of other companies they have invested in. Naturally, an investor with good experience in the specific industry of the proposed venture is very desirable. This can speed up the evaluation process. Quite frequently an investor will want to serve as a director of the venture or at least have the right to nominate a director. In some instances, the investor or investment group will want to control the board of directors. An interested, hardworking, and competent board of directors can be very helpful to them management of a new venture, and some investors can be very useful in obtaining competent people to serve as directors—often a very difficult and unrewarding task. Perhaps the most important characteristic of an investor, and the hardest for the entrepreneur to evaluate, is the willingness and ability of the investor to develop an understanding of the continuous problems and many potentials of a young company as well as an understanding of the entrepreneur. When such an investor does develop, the entrepreneur has someone he can turn to for a sympathetic and knowledgeable discussion of business and business-related personal problems that he cannot discuss with others in the company.

III THE ENTREPRENEUR AND THE LAW

Basic legal counsel for the entrepreneur comes from two sources: the corporate lawyer and the patent attorney. It is easy to gather names of potential attorneys for your company but quite another thing to find the one who is best suited to your needs. The main problem is that your business will not amount to a major portion of an attorney's work for several years. Consequently, he may not always provide the prompt and careful service that you require. You will need legal advice in many areas not directly associated with the formation of a business entity. For example, advice on many questions of simple business strategy can be offered by a lawyer. It is also valuable to have someone in your corner who is able and aggressive when you are negotiating a deal with investors.

From my own experience, I would suggest that you look for a bright young junior attorney in a large law firm. If he takes a personal interest in your activities, he can be very helpful. For his lack of experience he will be able to substitute the broad knowledge and experience of senior lawyers in his firm. Since rates for junior attorneys are less than for senior partners, you may be able to minimize legal fees. But the most important thing is to *choose a lawyer who is interested in you.* The size of his law firm is a significant, but secondary, issue. You can always change lawyers later if your company's needs change.

In Chapter 9, Edward A. Saxe covers five basic areas related to the formation of a new company: former employers, incorporation, agreements among founders, raising money, and agreements with investors.

Joseph Zallen, in Chapter 10, discusses patents, trademarks, and copyrights. As you relate this information to your own company's needs, you should be aware of changing attitudes toward patents. There was a time when they were considered of great significance in the creation of new technical companies. There is no question that patents still have value, but sophisticated venture capitalists have come to realize that no patent ever sold a single dollar's worth of product. Good management—producing and selling a product successfully—is more important. Furthermore, a great deal of money can be spent in the several stages of patent pursuit: the search, the development of the application, negotiations with the federal Patent Office, the filing of foreign patents if necessary, and, finally, prosecution of infringers of your patents. You should study the usefulness and necessity of every phase of the process before you begin.

William D. Putt

9 THE ENTREPRENEUR AND CORPORATE LAW

Edward A. Saxe*

This chapter deals with the legal problems encountered in organizing and financing a new venture, as well as the relationship between an entrepreneur and his legal advisor. Sound legal advice at the very beginning of your planning will enhance your position with sources of capital and may save you from making costly mistakes.

Choice of an Attorney

How do you find the right lawyer? Some entrepreneurs get names of lawyers from business associates, an accountant, an insurance man, a banker, or other professional acquaintances. When you have chosen someone highly recommended by people whose judgment you trust, meet with him to discuss your venture without making any commitment. Find out if and how he can help you. There is nothing unusual about interviewing a prospective attorney.

What are you looking for? Obviously, your attorney should be skilled in the area of business, or what is usually called "corporate law." Whether he is in practice by himself or a member of a firm, he should have had considerable experience

* Edward A. Saxe received his A.B. from Harvard College and his LL.B. from the Harvard Law School. He is currently a managing partner of Peabody, Brown, Rowley & Storey in Boston, Massachusetts.

working with new companies seeking venture capital. In addition, you will want someone who will agree to give you a reasonable amount of his time during your company's formative stages.

Since I am a member of a fairly large law firm, I naturally feel biased in this direction. I believe that a member of a medium-sized or large firm will be of greater assistance in the long run than an individual practitioner or an attorney in a small firm. Although you want a lawyer who will give you the time you need, it is also highly advantageous to have other lawyers in his firm available to you. They can work on your problems with your attorney and may be helpful to you when he is unavailable. Later on, when your company's needs change, a large law firm can provide specialization in areas such as real estate, litigation, taxation, labor and securities law, as well as general corporate work. Many small law practices cannot provide such specialization.

Before you finally settle on an attorney, discuss the question of legal fees with him. Many firms or attorneys will work on a contingency basis. In other words, if you are not able to raise the necessary capital to begin operations, you will not have to pay your lawyer anything except his out-of-pocket expenses. Whether or not an attorney will agree to this type of relationship will depend on several factors, including his estimate of the likelihood of your success in raising capital. If an entrepreneur already has sufficient capital to begin operations, an attorney may stipulate a minimum legal fee regardless of the success of the venture. Some attorneys will agree to accept company stock for their services or to take payment partly in cash and partly in stock. Larger law firms usually will not accept stock, however, since they have many partners and many clients and do not want to risk a conflict of interest. An attorney will normally base his charges on the amount of time he spends on your company's problems. Attorneys usually keep records of the amount of time spent on each matter and have a standard hourly rate. This will vary from approximately $45 to $100 per hour, depending on the skill, experience, and reputation of the attorney. It is difficult to estimate how many hours of work a new company will need. If you plan to raise a substantial amount of capital and need an attorney to help you through all the initial stages of your venture (incorporation, negotiations and agreements with investors, compliance with applicable securities laws, the drafting of all employment and other personnel agreements), you should expect legal costs of $5000–10,000. On the other hand, if you do not expect your attorney to spend large amounts of time helping you with your business plan or negotiating with investors, his fee will be approximately $500–1000 for organizing your business, preparing routine employment and other agreements, helping with the election of company officers and directors, preparing the bylaws, helping with the selection of a company name, and issuing the initial stock to the founders of your company. Filing fees for incorporating range from $50 to $150.

Extralegal Assistance from Your Attorney

The choice of a reputable attorney or law firm will enhance the credibility of your new company within the financial community. Your attorney may also be able to recommend contacts for sources of investment, an important aspect of raising capital. If he makes contacts for you himself, he will not charge a finder's fee, but his legal fee will probably be higher if the contact is successful.

Although entrepreneurs sometimes ask their attorney to serve as a director of their new company, the present tendency among lawyers is to avoid this type of relationship. This is particularly true while a company is still raising initial capital and before it becomes a profitable and stable operation. There are significant liabilities in being a director. Furthermore, a lawyer/director may be caught in a conflict of interest: his legal advice could be influenced by his liabilities as a director of the company. A good attorney will give you the business advice you require whether or not he is formally serving as a director of your company.

Relations with Your Present or Former Employer

As soon as you begin to develop your concept for a new business, it is important to find out if there are any legal impediments to your business plan. When entrepreneurs decide to compete with their present employers or to appropriate know-how or personnel from their employers, many legal questions have to be considered. A majority of the new ventures with which I have been associated have had to face problems in this area. One of the first things I explore with a new business group is the status of any patent, noncompetition, trade-secret, or employment agreements to which individual founders have been parties. It is necessary to determine if the entrepreneurs are legally free to embark on their venture. A noncompetition agreement between an entrepreneur and his present employer can be an absolute barrier, as could be employer's patent rights.

A typical employment agreement is contained in Exhibit 1, which also includes a noncompetition provision often used for key employees. (See exhibits at end of chapter.) The trade-secret and patent-assignment agreements shown in Exhibit 2 are more typical, however. These agreements prohibit the employee from disclosing or using secret and confidential information, such as formulas, special processes or techniques, and customer lists. Under patent agreements, inventions and discoveries related to the employer's business must be assigned to the employer. In some cases, this includes inventions conceived within a specified period after termination of employment. Even without a written agreement, the common law prohibits a person from disclosing or using certain secret and confidential information belonging to his former employer, although the restrictions imposed by the common law do not go as far as those imposed by the provisions of the agreement in Exhibit 1.

This is a very difficult area in which to make legal generalities. In rare instances, your employer may give you permission to proceed with your plan. Or you may decide to seek a declaratory judgment from the court, if you don't mind tipping your hand to your employer at an early date. If you are subject to restrictive agreements, you may decide to take a calculated risk and face the possibility of litigation with your employer, or former employer, hoping that a favorable settlement can be won. Although the trend of the law is to reduce the rights of employers against former employees, nondisclosure and noncompetition agreements are, in general, still enforceable and therefore cannot be ignored.

Often, when potential entrepreneurs begin discussions with me, their plans are still in the formulative stage, and they are still holding regular jobs. They usually want to continue their employment until their new venture is ready to begin operating, if they can. It is possible to do a certain amount of planning and even to seek capital during your free time, but while you are still employed, you are under an obligation not to compete with your employer. If you expect some litigation from your employer, the less you do while actually employed by him, the better your legal position will be. Ideally, you should resign at the beginning, so that you cannot be accused of soliciting potential customers, using your employer's resources, or "stealing" fellow employees while on the job. There is usually no prohibition against seeking to hire employees of your *former* employer unless this violates an existing written

employment agreement. In any event, you have to be prepared
to leave your employer once your plan is under way, since your
activities may be discovered when you initiate talks with
capital sources and distribute copies of your business plan. A
client of mine gave his business plan to the venture capital
division of a large bank. It was reviewed by the bank's board of
directors. Unfortunately for my client, one of the bank
directors was an attorney for the company that employed one
of the principal founders of the new company. Quite soon, the
entrepreneur was out of a job—well before the new company
was able to obtain its financing. As a general rule, I would
recommend against forming or incorporating your new business or taking any direct competitive action against your
employer until your employment has been terminated.

The greatest danger surrounding a legal dispute with your
employer, other than losing the suit, is the effect that actual or
potential litigation will have on capital sources. No investor
wants to have his funds wasted on long and expensive
litigation. More to the point, he will not invest in a company
that may not be able to function at all because of legal
prohibitions. With a number of my clients, investors have
refused to consider the investment situation if there is any
likelihood of lawsuits.

Choice of Business Entity

It is advisable to determine at a very early stage in your
planning what type of business entity your company will
become, preferably before investors are approached. This
enables the founders to obtain the tax advantages resulting
from an early issuance of stock.

Most new companies, particularly those involving more than
one founder, are established as corporations. This is the most
common type of business entity because it has the advantages

of limited liability, an established legal framework, and the flexibility to deal with investor groups, and because it permits agreements among the founders themselves. If you are in business by yourself, you may prefer a sole proprietorship. If there are only a few investors, you may choose a partnership or a limited partnership. Sometimes tax losses can be used by investors if a limited partnership is established. In such cases, the company can be established at a later date without adverse tax consequences. Occasionally, a partnership as well as a corporation is established. Then the partnership leases certain real or personal property to the corporation. Not only does this obtain certain tax advantages for the investors, who would own much of the equity in the limited partnership, but it also helps to protect the assets of the partnership from the claims of outside creditors of the corporation. If there are more than a few investors, however, you would normally establish a single corporation.

Place of Incorporation

If the corporate form is to be used, you must choose a state in which to incorporate. You may choose to incorporate in the state in which you are principally doing business. Or you may choose another state. The state of Delaware is the alternative most frequently chosen because (1) it has the most modern and flexible corporate laws regarding the issuance of stock, meetings of stockholders and directors, indemnification of officers and directors, and so forth; (2) its laws provide greater certainty than many other states; and (3) it has favorable tax laws.

If you are going to do business in one state only, it is usually advisable to incorporate in that state. Not only will your attorney be more familiar with the laws, but you will be able to take advantage of certain tax savings that are available to companies incorporated in the state in which they do business. On the other hand, if you plan to seek a large initial investment, are considering a public offering in the near future, and will be operating in several states, it may be to your advantage to incorporate in Delaware. If you decide to incorporate now in the state where you are operating, you may later reincorporate in Delaware if it better suits your company's needs.

Choice of a Company Name

Another matter to be considered in organizing a corporation is the choice of a business name. If you intend to do business in many states or on a national scale, you should verify that your company's name may be used wherever you go. I usually advise my clients to choose a name that is unique, not necessarily one that is symbolic of the industry in which they are engaged. This increases the likelihood that the name will be acceptable everywhere. You may also wish to verify the trademark availability of your company name. It is sometimes worthwhile, at a cost of about $100, to run a trademark and use-of-name search throughout the United States, or at least in the principal states in which you will be operating.

Tax Considerations

Once you have incorporated, you must decide immediately whether or not to file an election with the Internal Revenue Service to be treated as a "Subchapter S" corporation. Stockholders in a Subchapter S corporation are taxed directly on the company's net income, or net loss, in proportion to their stock ownership. In order to elect Subchapter S status, the corporation must have only one class of stock and no more than ten stockholders, all of whom must be *residents* of the

United States. Companies elect Subchapter S if they expect to
sustain a loss during the first years of business. Stockholders
can use these tax losses as a direct deduction against their other
income. This may mean little to the entrepreneur, since he will
probably have no outside income to offset the company's losses.
But this aspect of the Subchapter S election can be a very
important inducement to outside investors. In the early years,
it is sometimes desirable to increase investors' ownership in the
company, to provide them with greater tax losses and a
correspondingly greater tax benefit from the Subchapter S
plan.

Another plan may be adopted to minimize investors' economic risk: the "Section 1244 plan." Section 1244 stock is
common stock issued by a corporation in exchange for cash or
property. The equity capital of the corporation must be under
$500,000, and there must be no outstanding stock options.
Virtually every new corporation can meet these requirements.
The significance of the Section 1244 Plan, for federal income
tax purposes, is that any loss incurred on the stock is allowed as
a deduction against ordinary income, rather than being treated
as a capital loss (as would otherwise be the case). Since there
are no disadvantages to the Section 1244 stock plan, it should
be used whenever possible.

Election of Officers and Directors

Initially, you will have to select officers and directors from
among the founding group of your company, even though this
selection may change after investors have been admitted. As
will be discussed later in the chapter, investors may insist on
maintaining control over the choice of officers and directors
and the operations of the company. Even among the founders,
however, it is often desirable to divide the directors into two or
more groups so that control of the company is not dependent

on stock ownership. For example, if there are two founders who agree that one will have 70 percent ownership and the other 30 percent ownership, you can have inequality of ownership and yet permit equal voting control. This can be accomplished by having two separate classes of stock: one class, representing 30 percent of the stock, elects two directors; the other class, representing 70 percent of the stock, also elects two directors. Or you may choose another alternative: two classes of stock known as voting and nonvoting. Each founder may then have an equal number of voting shares but an unequal number of nonvoting shares.

Issuance of Stock to the Founders

The issuance of stock to the founders is important to the founders and to the Internal Revenue Service. You will not know ahead of time how much of the common stock of the company, as a percentage of ownership, the investors will insist on receiving in exchange for their investment, and it may seem easier to wait until arrangements with investors are negotiated before issuing stock to the founders. But from a tax standpoint, it is usually necessary to issue stock to the founders at a point well before the investors receive theirs. The reason for this is very simple. The founders will ordinarily pay only a nominal amount for their stock, compared to the amount paid by the investors. If stock is issued simultaneously to both the investors and the founders, at substantially different prices, the Internal Revenue Service can claim that the founders are receiving compensation in the form of "bargain price" stock. The founders will then be required to pay income tax on the difference between the "bargain price" and the price paid by the investors. To avoid this, stock in the new company should be issued to the founders as early as possible—at least a month or two before the investors receive theirs.

Sometimes a group of founders divides the ownership of stock equally. More usually, however, there are two or more key founders and a larger group of valuable, but less important, founder-employees. In this case, the key founders naturally expect to receive the bulk of the stock. For the remaining founder-employees, it is common to make provisions for the repurchase of their shares of stock at a nominal, book, or less-than-fair-market-value price if they do not remain with the new company for a specified length of time. These individuals may also be compensated through the use of stock options or other bonus arrangements. The tax and economic consequences of such arrangements are, of course, less favorable to them than the immediate issuance of stock, since the gain on a later disposition of such stock will be taxable as ordinary income rather than capital gain. In addition, the issuance of stock options will prevent the use of the Section 1244 stock plan discussed earlier.

Since the founders usually have very little capital of their own, they expect to purchase their stock for a nominal price. The investors, on the other hand, will probably want the founders to make a substantial financial commitment to the venture, thus ensuring that they will have the incentive to make the new company a success. The investors may demand that the founders pay as high a price for their stock as is within their means. On the assumption that the founders do not have cash or other available assets, they and their key employees may elect to purchase stock on an installment plan for a higher price than they could otherwise afford. The stock so purchased is known as "installment stock." Such an arrangement is permissible under the corporate statutes of many states (including Delaware). The total cost of the stock is usually payable over a five- or ten-year period, with only a modest interest rate. This arrangement constitutes a binding obligation on the founders. It is to their advantage, since it enables them to defer payment of most of the price until a time when the company will be more valuable.

In addition to committing cash and other personal resources in exchange for their stock, the founders may have know-how, patents, trade secrets, and other property, tangible or intangible, to contribute to the business. In such situations, the founders may transfer this property to the corporation in exchange for stock. Care must be taken to analyze the tax aspects of the transfer, in order to minimize or avoid any income taxes in connection with the exchange. Normally, if the property is transferred to the corporation as a capital contribution or in exchange for stock, there is no income tax to pay in connection with the transfer because it will become part of a tax-free incorporation. However, if the property is sold to the company or is exchanged for company notes, then income tax may be due on any gain, either capital gain or ordinary income. This will depend on the particular transaction. In any event, investors will insist that any assets, know-how, patents, trade secrets, and other property owned by the founders and essential to the business be legally transferred to the corporation before they commit their funds.

When the founders are determining their relative equity interests in the new company and the amount and form of their respective contributions in exchange for stock, they should also determine the distribution of voting power or voting control. The use of voting and nonvoting stock and two classes of directors has already been mentioned. The founders may also want to consider the use of a voting trust, or trusts, whereby one or more of the founders are trustees, with power to vote the stock owned by some or all of the remaining founders. The founders should also consider buy-out agreements among themselves, regardless of the agreements that may ultimately be made with the investors. For example, they may formally agree that in the event that any one of them should leave the company or die, the others would acquire his stock for a fixed price or a price to be determined by a particular formula. This will ensure that all the stock owned by the founders will be kept among the original group.

Employment Agreements

The founders of a new company should consider the advisability of employment agreements between some or all of them and their new company. Such employment agreements will usually be insisted upon—and in some cases their terms will be dictated—by the investors. They will usually cover not only employment but matters such as trade secrets and patent arrangements. In the case of key employees, the agreements will usually contain noncompetition provisions. Although the terms may later be dictated by the investors, the founders should negotiate terms among themselves and reach an understanding as to their relative positions, so that problems will not develop when definitive agreements with investors have to be made. Your attorney and other advisors can explain what compensation arrangements and other terms are likely to be required by investors. In general, a noncompetition agreement usually covers a substantial period of time, from one to three years after the termination of employment. Investors may also require that the founders sign a contract for a specific period of employment, perhaps from three to five years, in order to protect their investment. The investors cannot, even with such an agreement, legally coerce anyone to continue to work for the company, however.

Contacts with Investors

Initial contact with potential investors is usually made through a written business plan prepared by the founders of the new

company. You should take every reasonable precaution to
ensure that your plan contains no materially false or misleading statements.

Your initial financing may come from a venture capital group
or from a number of private investors. When you are seeking
financing from individual investors, you ordinarily prepare
what is known as a "private placement memorandum." This
should describe the new company in great detail: its proposed
activities, its management, the background of the founders, the
nature of the securities offered for investment, and the
proposed terms of the offering. In short, the private placement
memorandum should include all the information found in a
regular prospectus prepared for a registered public offering.
This memorandum will be used to offer the securities of the
new company to, and solicit investments from, various private
investors. As such, it will constitute an offering of securities by
the new company and will therefore be subject to the
provisions of all federal and state securities laws. These laws
impose liability on anyone who offers or sells securities by
means of false or misleading statements. The memorandum
should be prepared very carefully. In particular, any projections included should be clearly supported by reliable information.

Securities law is not always easy to understand. The rules that
render it unlawful for any person to sell any security by means
of a false or misleading statement are relatively straightforward. The fundamental principle is simply that fraud, which
includes for this purpose not only untruths but also half-truths
and material omissions, is unlawful in connection with the offer
or sale of securities, and that anyone who engages in such fraud
will become an insurer, to the purchasers, of the price paid for
the securities. There is another, more complex aspect to the
securities law, however. The federal securities law (the Securities Act of 1933) and the securities laws of most of the states

render it unlawful for any person to offer or sell a security unless (1) a registration statement or similar form is first filed with the appropriate authorities (such as the Securities and Exchange Commission); or (2) the type of security involved, or the particular form of the transaction, is exempt from the registration requirements. The purpose of these laws is to ensure full and fair disclosure in connection with any public offering of securities. Most new companies seek exemption from registration requirements and must take great care to avoid the violation of securities laws in seeking capital. We turn, therefore, to an analysis of the exemptions on which a new company will most often rely.

The Private Placement Exemption

The private placement exemption, most commonly used by new companies, covers transactions that do not involve a public offering. Under the terms of this exemption, an offering of securities may be made to *a small number* of investors without being considered a public offering. It should be most carefully noted that in determining whether or not an offering is public, it is the *number of offeries,* not the number of ultimate purchasers, which is relevant. Although there is no particular number that is controlling, the offering does not usually qualify for a private placement exemption if more than 25 offerees are involved.

There are some other requirements for a private placement exemption. In order for a transaction to be eligible, the offerees must be "sophisticated investors" who have access to the type of information that would normally be included in a prospectus for a public offering—in other words, people who are not in need of the protection afforded by registration. Furthermore, the investors must agree to purchase the securities "for investment," and not with the intention of reoffering them to other persons. This requirement has given rise to the practice of obtaining "investment letters" from investors. When the requirements for the private placement exemption have been met, the offering may be made within one state or in a number of states.

The Securities and Exchange Commission has recently proposed Rule 146, which, if adopted, would clarify and expand somewhat the above-described rules for a private placement exemption.

Most state securities laws, called "Blue Sky laws," contain an exemption from their registration requirements which corresponds to the private placement exemption covered in the federal statute, although it is often phrased in quite different terms. For example, many states exempt "casual or isolated sales" of securities.

The Intrastate Offering Exemption

Your company may want to make an offering of its securities to such a large number of investors that you are not eligible for the private placement exemption. At the same time, your potential investors may all be located within a single state. In such a case, you should consider the intrastate offering exemption. This is an exemption from registration with the Securities and Exchange Commission and is available when securities are offered and sold only to persons who are residents of a single state. This must be the state where the company is incorporated and doing business. Thus, if your new company is incorporated in Minnesota and doing business there, you could, under federal securities laws, offer and sell securities to an unlimited number of potential investors in Minnesota without federal registration. If your company is located in and doing business in Minnesota but incorporated in Delaware, you do not qualify for the intrastate offering exemption.

This exemption is very difficult to comply with. If an offer is made to even one individual outside the state, the exemption will be lost. When an offering is made to a large number of people, some of whom may be strangers to you, it is very hard to ensure that the securities will not be inadvertently offered to a nonresident. Furthermore, "legal residence," for the purpose of the exemption, is not a clear-cut concept. Some offerees who think they are residents of the state may, in the terms of the exemption, turn out to be residents of another state. Finally, the purchasers of the securities must take the securities with a commitment not to resell them, similar to the commitment made by the purchasers in a private placement. If any one of the purchasers resells the securities within a short time to persons who are not residents of the state, the exemption will be lost. For all these reasons, reliance on the intrastate offering exemption, despite its apparent simplicity, is dangerous. In almost any case in which you can safely rely on the intrastate offering exemption, you can also safely rely on the private placement exemption, and the latter is preferable.

The federal securities laws exempt intrastate offerings because state, rather than federal, regulation seems more appropriate for such offerings. But it is important to realize that if an offering is made to a large number of potential investors in one state, you still must register under the Blue Sky laws of that state, even though you qualify for the federal intrastate offering exemption. For every offering of securities, in other words, you must study both federal and state registration regulations.

Failure to Comply with Securities Laws

If your company makes an offering of securities without registration and the offering does not meet the terms of an exemption, this is, by definition, a violation of the federal and/or state securities laws. When registration requirements are violated, the company issuing the securities, and its officers and directors as well, will be subject to civil liability to the purchasers of the securities. The investors will have the right to return the securities and demand the return of their money. In addition, if the violation is found to have been willful, the officers, directors, and other persons involved in the violation may be subject to criminal penalties.

If a company has failed to comply with all the conditions of an exemption at the time of an initial offering of securities, it will be in serious trouble if it ever plans to register for a public offering later on. Many new companies raise their initial capital in a private placement or an intrastate offering, with the intention of making a registered public offering after the company has begun operations. For the public offering, of course, the company must file a registration statement with the Securities and Exchange Commission. If the Commission discovers that there has been, or may have been, an earlier violation of the federal securities laws, not only will they begin an investigation, but they may insist that the company make a rescission offer (an offer to take back the stock and return the purchase price) to the stockholders who purchased securities in the earlier offering.

"Regulation A" and Registered Public Offerings

Most new companies do not obtain their initial financing through any type of public offering, although sometimes there is a market for "hot new issues." Many obtain initial financing in a private placement with the intention of making a public offering later to raise additional capital. It is usually the hope of investors that a public market will be created for the stock of the company. Consequently, you should know something about this aspect of raising capital. There are basically two types of public offering: a "Regulation A" offering and a fully registered, or "regular," public offering.

A Regulation A offering is a public offering of securities pursuant to the "small offering" exemption under the federal securities laws. The fundamental condition for a Regulation A offering is that it does not exceed $500,000. An offering for $500,000 or less is technically exempt from the registration requirements of the federal securities laws, but I have not grouped it with the private placement exemption and the intrastate offering exemption because certain information does have to be filed with the Securities and Exchange Commission. For a Regulation A offering, a company must file an offering circular (similar to a regular prospectus) with the Commission. But the offering circular and other required documents are filed with the local office of the Commission rather than the central office in Washington, D.C. The time taken by the Commission staff to review a Regulation A offering circular and other documents is considerably less than the time required in a regular public offering. A Regulation A offering is also less expensive than a regular public offering in terms of legal, accounting, and filing fees and is much simpler in many other respects. Sometimes the offering can be made within two or three months after the new company begins the preparation of the offering circular. A Regulation A offering may be handled by an underwriter or group of underwriters in substantially the same manner as a regular public offering. But it is not uncommon for a company to carry out the offering on its own.

If your company needs to raise more than $500,000, it will have to make a full-scale regular public offering. The first step is usually a negotiation with an investment banking firm to arrange for an underwriting of the public offering. Once an underwriter has expressed definite interest, the company must prepare a registration statement including detailed financial information and a fairly comprehensive description of the company and its products. The management of the company will have to spend time with the company's lawyers and accountants to prepare the registration statement. When the registration statement is filed with the Securities and Exchange Commission in Washington, D.C., the staff of the Commission will review it and make extensive comments on it. Your company must also comply with the Blue Sky laws of the states in which its securities will be offered. Various forms and other documents must be filed with the appropriate authorities in each state. Registration proceedings may take six months or more. Various problems may create delays. And finally, when all the work has been done, the underwriters may decide that conditions in the stock market are such that the timing of the offering should be postponed. In spite of the time involved, however, a full-scale registered public offering is the most feasible method for raising a substantial amount of capital.

Agreements with Investors

Let us assume that the founders of a new company decide to raise their initial capital through a private placement, thereby qualifying for the private placement exemption from the federal securities laws. The first and most significant topic in the negotiations with potential investors is the question of what percentage of the common stock (the basic ownership of the company) will be required by the investors in exchange for their investment. A related question is whether securities other than, or in addition to, common stock will be sold to the investors. For example, it is not uncommon for the company to sell a package to the investors consisting of common stock and preferred stock or debentures. The preferred stock or debentures may have warrants attached to purchase common stock or may be convertible into common stock. (See Chapter 8.) Assuming that these basic matters can be resolved, counsel for the company and for the venture capital group or groups will then begin the preparation of a written agreement. The agreement will contain provisions setting forth not only the basic terms of the investment deal but also any other terms and conditions required by the investors. For example, the investors may insist on the right to elect one or more representatives to the board of directors of the company. They may require the company to maintain life insurance on its key founders. They may impose limitations on the company with respect to capital expenditures, additional borrowings, payment of dividends, the sale of assets, and/or the issuance of additional stock. The investors may also insist that they be given the right to buy stock on a pro rata (proportional distribution) basis if any additional sales of stock are made by the company, in order to maintain their percentage of ownership.

Since the investment will be made in the form of a private placement, the securities received by the investors will be restricted; that is, they may not be freely resold by the investors (as explained in the discussion of the private placement exemption). Of course, investors would like their investment to become liquid eventually, and they will be interested in having the company make a public offering. To secure the right to sell their shares on the market if and when the company goes public, the investors will negotiate terms concerning their right to have their shares registered with the Securities and Exchange Commission. Such registration rights take a number of different forms. The investors may be given rights to a "piggyback" registration, which will entitle them to have their shares registered if, within a certain period of time, the company should file a registration statement with the Securities and Exchange Commission. Piggyback registration rights are usually the least burdensome type from the entrepreneur's point of view. They require only that the company register the shares belonging to investors when the company (or stockholders of the company) makes a registered offering. However, even

piggyback registration rights may prove troublesome for the
company when it decides to make a public offering. For
example, the underwriters of the public offering may object to
the investors selling their shares on the market at the same time
as the underwritten offering. Therefore, the company should
try to subject any piggyback registration rights to certain
restrictions: (1) that the investors may not sell their shares
within a certain time after the registration statement becomes
effective; and (2) that the investors may not make any sale of
stock if the underwriters of a public offering object.

Investors are not often satisfied to have only piggyback
registration rights. They may insist on the right to have their
shares registered even if the company does not decide to make
a public offering and the right to create a public market for
company stock within a certain period of time. Or they may
insist on an absolute right to have their shares registered, at
their request, any time after a year from the date of their
investment. Companies do not usually like to grant extensive
registration rights to investors because they may then be forced
to file a registration statement and to go public before they are
ready. If the investors insist on having such rights, however, the
company may have no choice. In connection with registration
rights, there is the question of who will bear the expense
associated with a registered public offering—the investors or
the company. In general, the company bears the expense of an
initial offering, whether it is initiated by the company itself or
by the investors. In many cases, the company has to carry the
expenses of subsequent offerings as well.

Your company should study terms required by potential
investors very carefully: some agreements may produce unexpected repercussions. In most cases, you will have to weigh
imperfect terms against your need for capital. Unless a client is
extremely confident that the "right" investor will eventually
appear, I usually advise him to accept terms that are

reasonably fair and close to his minimum goals—in the hope that his company's success will improve his bargaining position and enable him to negotiate improved terms within a reasonable time.

Exhibit 1

EMPLOYMENT AGREEMENT

THIS AGREEMENT, made as of the date last written below, by and between   , a Massachusetts corporation (hereinafter referred to as the "Company"), and   (hereinafter referred to as the "Executive").

WITNESSETH:

WHEREAS the Company is in the business of

                        and kindred and related subjects and matters; and

WHEREAS the Company has elected the Executive as a Vice President.

NOW THEREFORE the following is agreed:

1. The Executive agrees to devote all of his time and efforts to the performance of such duties as are consistent with and required of him and which may be assigned to him from time to time in connection therewith by the Board of Directors of the Company. He also agrees that during the term hereof he will not, directly or indirectly, alone or as a partner, employee, consultant, officer, director, stockholder (except as a holder of one percent (1%) or less of the issued stock in any company whose stock is publicly traded) or in any other capacity with any other organization, entity or business, be engaged in any commercial activity without approval of the Board of Directors of the Company.

2. Unless earlier terminated as provided in this Agreement, the term of employment shall be three (3) years from

3. For all the services to be rendered by the Executive in any capacity hereunder including services for the Company or any subsidiary or affiliate as an officer, director, member of any committee, consultant or any other duties assigned him by the executive committee, or by the directors of the Company, the Company agrees to pay the Executive a salary of not less than
                                        per annum, payable in
equal monthly installments at the end of each month. The Board of Directors may, during the term hereof, authorize such additional compensation by way of salary, bonus or otherwise as it deems appropriate.

4. The Executive shall be entitled to such vacation time and such fringe benefits as are commonly granted to persons of comparable standing in the employ of the Company.

5. As a further inducement to the Executive to enter into this Agreement and to provide a means of his obtaining a proprietary interest in the Company and to increase his incentive, the Company hereby grants to the Executive an option to purchase in cash up to five thousand (5,000) shares of the stock of the Company for such price and upon such terms as are specified in the Stock Option Agreement marked "A" which is attached hereto and made part of this Agreement.

6. The Executive agrees that the Company, in its discretion, may apply for and procure in its own name and for its own benefit, life insurance in any amount or amounts considered advisable and that he shall have no right, title or interest therein, and further, agrees to submit to any medical or other examination and to execute and deliver any application or other instrument in writing, reasonably necessary to effectuate such insurance.

7. The Executive acknowledges that prior to his employment by the Company he had no knowledge of the formulas, processes, methods of manufacture, general know-how or business confidences of the Company. The Executive agrees

not to divulge to anyone, either during or after the termination of his employment, any information acquired by him concerning such formulas, processes, methods of manufacture, general know-how, business confidences, or other trade secrets of the Company. Upon the termination of his employment the Executive agrees forthwith to deliver up to the Company all notebooks, data or other materials of any kind relating to research or experiments conducted by him or relating to the products, formulas, processes, methods of manufacture, general know-how or business confidences of the Company.

8. The Executive shall promptly disclose in writing to the Company all inventions, discoveries and improvements, whether or not patentable, devised by him, either solely or jointly with others, while in the employ of the Company. He also agrees to communicate to the Company promptly in writing all inventions, discoveries and improvements, whether or not patentable, which he devises, either solely or jointly, during the period of one (1) year following the termination of this Agreement, however occurring, which relate to any of the services rendered, or any of the fields, programs and/or products engaged in, produced by or under development by the Company prior to or at the time of such termination. The Executive hereby transfers and assigns to the Company all right, title and interest in and to any and all inventions, discoveries and improvements covered by this paragraph, and any and all domestic and foreign patent rights therein and any renewals thereof. On request of the Company, the Executive shall execute from time to time during or after the termination of his employment, such further instruments, including without limitation applications for letters patent and assignments thereof, as may be deemed necessary or desirable by the Company to effectuate the provisions of this Agreement. All expenses of filing or prosecuting any patent applications shall be borne solely by the Company, but the Executive shall

cooperate in filing and/or prosecuting any such applications.

9. The Executive agrees that for a period of two (2) years following the termination of his employment, however occurring, he will not enter the employ of any person, firm or corporation engaged in a similar line of business in competition with the Company, nor himself engage during such period, directly or indirectly, alone or as a partner, consultant, officer, director, stockholder (except as a holder of one percent (1%) or less of the issued stock for any company whose stock is publicly traded), or in any other capacity, in any such business in competition with the Company. The foregoing restrictions shall be binding throughout each of the New England States and in any other state or foreign country in which the Company or its subsidiaries is selling, has sold, or has made definite plans to sell its product or services during the Executive's employment. The parties hereto recognize that the services to be performed by the Executive are special and unique, and that by reason of this employment the Executive will acquire confidential information as aforesaid. It is agreed that any breach of this Agreement by the Executive shall entitle the Company, in addition to any other legal remedies available to it, to apply to any court of competent jurisdiction to enjoin any violation of this Agreement. For purposes hereof, a business will be deemed competitive if it involves the production, manufacture or distribution of any products or rendition of any services similar to products and services produced, manufactured or distributed by the Company or any of its subsidiaries.

10. The Executive represents and warrants that he is free to enter into this Agreement, that he has not made and will not make any agreements in conflict with this Agreement, and will not disclose to the Company, nor use for the Company's benefit, any trade secrets or confidential information which is the property of any party other than the Company.

11. In the event that during the employment period the Executive shall be disabled from rendering services hereunder for six (6) consecutive months, the Board of Directors of the Company may terminate employment thereunder after sixty (60) days written notice, and in that event the Executive shall be paid through the said period of sixty (60) days but shall have no additional rights under this Agreement which have not accrued before the end of said period. If, however, prior to the date specified in said notice, the Executive's illness or incapacity shall have terminated and he shall have resumed his duties hereunder, the Executive shall be entitled to continue his employment hereunder as though such notice had not been given.

12. In the event of the Executive's death during the term of this Agreement, it shall terminate immediately and the Executive's legal representatives shall be entitled to receive the compensation due the Executive through the last day of the calendar month in which his death shall have occurred.

13. In addition to any other provisions herein contained regarding the termination of this Agreement, the Company may terminate the same upon fourteen (14) days written notice if the Executive shall, during the course of his association or employment with the Company, show any disloyalty to the Company or if his personal conduct shall reflect adversely upon the Company or its business. In the event of termination as aforesaid, the Company shall be obligated to pay the Executive only such compensation as is due him up to the date of termination.

14. The waiver by either party or a breach of any provisions of this Agreement shall not operate as or be construed as a waiver of any prior or subsequent breach thereof.

15. The rights and benefits of the Company under this Agreement shall be transferable, and all covenants and agreements hereunder as shall inure to the benefit of and be enforceable by, or against its successors and assigns.

16. Any disagreement or controversy between the parties to this Agreement shall be determined by arbitration as follows: On ten (10) days written notice by either party to the other, each of them shall designate an arbitrator, and a third arbitrator shall be selected by the two so designated. In the event that either party fails to designate an arbitrator within ten (10) days following notice, or in the event of their inability or failure to agree upon a third, within ten (10) days following their designation, such selection shall be made by the Company's legal counsel. The decision in writing of any two of the arbitrators designated or selected in accordance with this paragraph shall be conclusive on both parties.

17. Any and all notices referred to herein shall be sufficient if furnished in writing and sent by registered mail to the appropriate party at his or its last known address.

18. If any portion or provision of this Agreement shall to any extent be invalid or unenforceable, the remainder of this Agreement, or the application of such portion or provision in circumstances other than those as to which it is held invalid or unenforceable, shall not be affected thereby and each portion and provision of this Agreement shall be valid and be enforceable to the fullest extent permitted.

19. This instrument shall represent the entire agreement between the parties hereto, any other or prior understandings, agreements and contracts being hereby canceled without any further liability whatsoever on either part. No modification or amendment to this Agreement will be effective unless expressed in a subsequent written document executed by both parties hereto.

IN WITNESS WHEREOF the parties hereto have hereunto set their hands and seals as of the   day of   19

By———————————————————

—————————————————————

Exhibit 2

PATENT AND CONFIDENTIAL INFORMATION
AGREEMENT

In consideration of my employment or continued employment by   (the "Employer"),
and for other valuable consideration, receipt of which is
acknowledged, I agree with Employer as follows:

1. During the period of my employment by the Employer, I
agree to devote my best efforts and full time to further the
interest of the Employer and I shall not, directly or indirectly,
alone or as a partner, employee, consultant, officer, director or
stockholder (except as a holder of one (1) percent or less of the
issued stock in any company whose stock is publicly traded) of
any other organization, entity, or business, be engaged in any
commercial activity without approval of the Board of Directors
of the Employer.

2. I recognize that by reason of my employment with the
Employer I will be engaged in, have contact with, and gain
knowledge of information, developments, research projects,
manufacturing and trade secrets, know-how and business
confidences relating to, and concerned with, the past, present
and future business operations, products and policies of the
Employer, its suppliers, customers and other persons, and,
accordingly, I agree to hold as secret and confidential any and
all information disclosed to me by the Employer, or which I
may learn of by virtue of my employment with the Employer. I
agree not to use such information for my own benefit or to
disclose or to use such information for the benefit of others,
both during the period of my employment and thereafter
following the termination of my employment, without the
written consent of the Employer, as long as such information is

not public knowledge. Upon the termination of my employment for any reason, I shall not take with me any originals or copies of any drawings, other documents, developments or pre-production models containing confidential information.

3. I agree to communicate to the Employer promptly, in writing, all inventions, discoveries, and improvements, whether or not patentable, which I may conceive or make, either solely or jointly with others, in any field and of any products, during the period of my employment with Employer. I also agree to communicate to the Employer promptly in writing, all inventions, discoveries, and improvements whether or not patentable, which I may conceive or make, either solely or jointly with others, during the period of one (1) year following the termination of this Agreement which directly relate to any of the fields, programs and products engaged in, produced by or under development by Employer prior to or at the time of such termination. I agree to take whatever steps are requested by the Employer toward securing patent or other legal protection on such inventions, discoveries and improvements in any and all countries, and further agree to assign the entire right, title and interest in the same, on request by the Employer, and in all patents and patent applications related thereto, to the Employer at any time, either during the period of my employment or thereafter, in the form of an assignment attached hereto as Exhibit "A", or such other document form as counsel for the Employer shall reasonably request. It is understood by and between the parties that all necessary costs of making such assignments and procuring such patents shall be paid for solely by the Employer.

One (1) year after I have made a disclosure to Employer (under foregoing provisions of this paragraph 3), which would be adequate for the filing of a proper U. S. patent application thereon, or within six (6) months after the subject matter of such disclosure has been either published anywhere or placed in public use or on sale in the United States, whichever is earlier, Employer shall, at my written request, state whether Employer intends to file a patent application on such disclosure, and if thereupon the Employer has either stated to me that it does not intend to file such U. S. patent application or, having stated its intention to file such patent application, does not file same within one (1) year following such statement of intention then I may file such U. S. patent application (and any corresponding foreign patent applications) at my own expense during the next one (1) year period. Any patent application filed by me under the terms of this paragraph shall be for my own benefit, subject to a royalty-free, nonexclusive, life-term license reserved to Employer under and with respect to all U. S. and foreign patent applications so filed and patents so obtained by me, and such license shall include the right of Employer to incorporate the subject matter of such application and/or patent in any design submitted by it to any of its customers or prospective customers and to incorporate same in any product made or manufactured by or on behalf of any other corporation affiliated with Employer.

4. I further agree to keep, maintain and make available to the Employer complete and up-to-date written records including, but not limited to, notebooks, reports, drawings and the like, of my inventions and improvements relating to Employer's programs, processes and products, which records shall be and remain the property of the Employer. All such records and the documents in my possession, and being the property of the Employer, shall be submitted to the Employer promptly upon the termination of my employment for whatever reason.

5. I represent and warrant that I am free to enter into this Agreement, that I have not made and will not make any agreements in conflict with this Agreement, and will not

disclose to the Employer, nor use for the Employer's benefit any trade secrets or confidential information which is the property of any other party now or hereafter in my possession.

6. The waiver by Employer of my breach of any provision of this Agreement shall not operate as or be construed as a waiver of any subsequent breach thereof.

7. The interpretation, construction and application of this Agreement shall be governed by Massachusetts law. This Agreement may be enforced in law or equity.

8. If any portion or provision of this Agreement shall to any extent be invalid or unenforceable, the remainder of this Agreement, or the application of such portion or provision in circumstances other than those as to which it is held invalid or unenforceable, shall not be affected thereby and each portion and provision of this Agreement shall be valid and be enforceable to the fullest extent permitted.

EXECUTED in duplicate under seal as of the   day of
        ,19   .

_____

Receipt Acknowledged:

By:_____

Exhibit A of Patent and Confidential
Information Agreement

ASSIGNMENT

I, _____ of _____ in consid-
eration of One Dollar and other valuable consideration
paid to _____ by   ,
a corporation of Massachusetts, having its principal place
of business at
Massachusetts, the receipt of which is hereby acknowledged, do hereby sell, assign and transfer unto said
                                                its successors and assigns,
the entire interest for the United States of America and all
foreign countries in a certain invention or improvement in
                                   (executed by   of even date
                                   (herewith and about to be filed
described in an application (Serial Number _____
                                   (filed on _____
in the United States Patent Office, and in all letters Patent of
the United States and all foreign countries which may or shall
be granted on said invention, or any parts thereof, or on said
application, or any divisional, continuing, reissue or other
applications based to the extent thereon. And _____ agree, for
_____ and _____ executors and administrators,
with said corporation and its successors and assigns but at its or
their expense and charges, hereafter to execute all applications,
amended specifications, deeds or other instruments, and to do
all other acts, reasonably necessary or proper to secure the
grant of Letters Patent in the United States and in all other
countries to said corporation, with specifications and claims in
such form as shall be reasonably approved by the counsel of
said corporation and to vest and confirm in said corporation,
its successors and assigns, the legal title to all such patents.

And _____ do hereby authorize and request the Commissioner of Patents of the United States to issue such Letters Patent as shall be granted upon said application or applications based thereon to said corporation, its successors and assigns.

WITNESS _____ hand and seal this _____ day of _____, 19 .

STATE OF _____)

) ss:

COUNTY OF _____)

Then personally appeared before me _____ , who, being duly sworn, acknowledged that _____ executed the foregoing instrument and that the statements herein set forth are true.

Notary Public

My commission expires:

10 PRODUCT PROTECTION

Joseph Zallen*

According to a 1964 decision by the U.S. Supreme Court, neither a federal nor a state court can prohibit the copying of an article or award damages for such copying when the article is unpatented or uncopyrighted. Without a patent or copyright, in other words, you cannot prevent a competitor from copying your product down to the last detail. Not all patents are alike. Some give limited, others very broad, coverage. Some patents, even though narrow, are difficult to circumvent. Others, even some that have very broad coverage, can be easily avoided. Many products cannot be patented. Even in marginal situations, however, I believe that it is important to apply for a patent if your product is new and has commercial value.

For the entrepreneur, a patent is a valuable piece of property, especially in dealing with investors. In fact, many investors are reluctant to invest capital in a company if it does not have a patent for its product or if a patent application has not been filed. Investors fear that larger, well-financed companies will be able to capture the market as soon as a small company has created it. A patent is also a basis for deriving revenue. An inventor can license or sell his invention if he chooses not to start a company of his own. Furthermore, a company owning a

* Joseph Zallen received his S.B. degree from M.I.T. and his J.D. degree from Northeastern University School of Law. He is a member of the bar of the U.S. Supreme Court, the U.S. Patent Office, Massachusetts, and Florida.

patent that it cannot exploit has the legal right to obtain revenue from royalties or from rent or sale of patent rights.

Most technically trained people can understand the subject matter of a patent and can determine the extent of its usefulness. Nevertheless, when obtaining a patent, deciding whether to seek a patent, preparing a license agreement, investigating validity or infringement, or pursuing litigation, it is advisable to utilize the services of a patent lawyer. The patent lawyer you select should have no conflict of interest with other clients he represents and should be qualified to represent you in both the U.S. Patent Office and the courts. In addition, he should have sufficient scientific or technical training to understand your speciality area. You can obtain information on particular patent lawyers from the *Martindale-Hubbell Law Directory* (Martindale-Hubbell, Inc., Summit, New Jersey). A good approach is to discuss the technical merits of your product with a prospective patent attorney. Other entrepreneurs may be able to help you in recommending a patent attorney.

The Patent Search

In the United States alone, about 3,750,000 patents have already been issued, and the patents continue to be issued at the rate of about 70,000 each year. U.S. patents are classified in over 400 general classes, each with hundreds of subclasses. The number and variety of patents make it virtually impossible for a scientist, engineer, inventor, or businessman to know from his own experience and reading whether his new product infringes someone else's patent. It is advisable, therefore—if the cost is not out of line—to subject new products to a patent search. The Search Room in the U.S. Patent Office is the only place where patents are arranged according to class and subclass. The collections of patents in public libraries throughout the United States are organized chronologically and provide no means for searching according to subject matter. Anyone can make a personal examination of the documents in the Search Room at the Patent Office in Alexandria, Virginia, but it is a laborious, time-consuming task. A familiar compromise is to have a Washington, D.C., associate of your patent attorney send you the patents that seem to have general relevance. You can then evaluate the technical disclosures in each and can help your patent attorney to decide whether your product infringes an existing patent and whether your new product itself is patentable. In certain fields there are companies that provide abstracts from patents—for example, *Chemical Abstracts,* for patents in the field of chemistry. Once a company has been in business for several years, it should have built up a comprehensive collection of patents issued within its limited sphere of interest. It is then sometimes possible for the company to evaluate its new products by referring to this patent collection if it has been constantly updated.

The search for infringement is slightly different from the search for patentability. A patent has a life-span of 17 years. Infringement searches are therefore limited to the 17 years preceding the search. There is one problem that cannot be avoided by even the most careful and comprehensive search: someone else may have a pending patent application for a product similar to yours. The Patent Office does not grant access to pending patent applications, and many are pending for several years. As a result, there is the possibility that a patent covering your product might be issued to another person some time *after* you have completed your search. If this happens, the law does permit you to introduce evidence that you were the first inventor, although the burden of proof is severe. For this reason, it is good practice for an inventor to keep detailed, dated, and witnessed written reports of his experiments and results. The key to success in such a contest is the ability to produce a witness who is knowledgeable in your field and who can testify that he or she actually saw you successfully perform your invention. (This is discussed in greater detail in a later section of this chapter.)

Trade Secrets

A trade secret is no substitute for a patent. A patent gives you the legal right to exclude anybody from making the product or using the process covered by the patent. A trade secret is simply information that a person or company keeps confidential. If a third person discovers or duplicates a trade secret without violating any confidence, that third party is entitled to use that trade secret. A competitor cannot hire your employee in order to learn that trade secret, but he is not forbidden to use all scientific and technical means at his disposal to determine what your trade secret is. To maintain a trade secret, you must have comprehensive security. If you initiate court proceedings in which violation of a trade secret is involved, you are generally required to show that you (1) informed all your employees that the product or method was a trade secret; (2) did not allow outsiders to have access to the trade secret; (3) used secure locks and similar barriers to protect your trade secret; and (4) have never divulged the trade secret to any third party. Since it is hard to prove what a trade secret is, you should put it in writing, if possible, and keep the document in a secure place. Even when all reasonable precautions are taken, however, courts sometimes hold that particular trade secrets are not substantially different from "what everyone knows" in the trade.

Most court cases involving trade secrets arise from suits brought by companies against present or former employees. In order to prove the existence of a trade secret, companies usually require each employee to sign a document acknowledging the existence of a trade secret and agreeing not to discuss it outside the company. When an employee who has signed such a document goes to work for a competitor, his original employer often suspects trade secret violation and considers bringing suit. The results of such suits vary. When employees have stolen written records or samples and delivered them to a competitor, the court has no trouble finding that a trade secret has been violated. When an employee has simply gone to work for a competitor, however, the courts are reluctant to interfere, primarily because of the overriding doctrine that a person is entitled to use his knowledge and skills to make a living.

In successful trade secret litigation, the penalties are severe. Two engineers employed by Sperry-Rand Corp. left to work for Electronic Concepts, Inc. While employed by Sperry-Rand they had developed a slotted array radar antenna that required special production techniques. An important part of the techniques was the manufacturing tolerances set forth in a special drawing. Both engineers had signed agreements at Sperry-Rand that they would not divulge confidential information. When they went to work for Electronic Concepts, they took with them not only the special drawing but also many other papers and documents relating to the antenna. Electronic Concepts then underbid Sperry-Rand for a government contract to make the antenna. The U.S. District Court in Richmond, Virginia, found a trade secret violation and awarded $631,012 compensatory damages and $185,000 in punitive damages to Sperry-Rand (Sperry-Rand Corp. v. Electronic Concepts, Inc., et al., 170 USPQ 410, Oct. 15, 1970). The amount was reduced on appeal to $400,000.

Information Contained in Patents

A patent, whether issued in the United States or in a foreign country, usually includes a description of the invention, followed by a statement concerning the scope of the invention. Drawings are required whenever there is a mechanical device, and these drawings must provide sufficient detail so that a reader knowledgeable in the field could construct a similar device. There is no requirement that the drawings be working drawings, however. In the United States, not only must a patent contain a broad description of the invention, but it is required to show at least one detailed example of the invention. Furthermore, in a U.S. patent, the statement concerning the scope of the invention—referred to as the "claims"—must be very carefully worded. It is the information contained in the claims that determines whether or not there has been an infringement on a patent. The claims are the numbered pseudoparagraphs that appear at the end of a patent. The main written portion of a U.S. patent is often referred to as "the specification." The patents and publications cited after the claims are those patents which the Patent Office studied before issuing the patent. In the heading of the patent, the name of the inventor is given, as well as the name of any company to which the patent has been assigned. The heading also gives the date of issuance of the patent and the filing date of the application or of any earlier related applications.

Filing a Patent Application

A patent is obtained by filing an application in accordance with Sections 101, 102, and 103 of Title 35 of the U.S. Code. These provisions require that the invention for which the patent is sought must be: (1) new and useful; (2) original with the inventor; (3) not anticipated by any existing patent or printed publication; (4) not on sale or in public use in the United States more than one year prior to filing the application; and (5) not obvious. After a patent application has been filed, it is thoroughly reviewed by an examiner in the Patent

Office. The examiner makes an independent search to decide whether a patent should be granted. If he rejects the application, he sends a written communication to the applicant which gives the reasons for the rejection and cites the prior patents and publications he has considered in making his decision. The applicant has the right to reply with arguments and evidence and can very often convince the examiner that the claims as originally presented, or as amended, should be allowed. This exchange of correspondence is often referred to as "patent prosecution." If the examiner decides that the patent is acceptable, the Patent Office issues an official notice. This calls upon the applicant to pay the issue fee, and upon payment he receives the patent. It will be in effect for 17 years from its date of issue. If the examiner does not accept the patent, the applicant can appeal the decision within the Patent Office and also to the courts. The period between the filing date of a patent application and the date of issue averages from two to three years.

Understanding Claims

There are several types of claim: a *composition,* such as an antibiotic, dye, plastic, or adhesive; a *product,* such as a lamp, golf club, or boat; a *machine,* such as a computer, reclining chair, or engine; a *method,* such as the production of foam plastic, the coating of cloth, or the treating of asthma. The language of a claim is interpreted in its ordinary sense whenever feasible. Since there is often some question about the meaning of words contained within the claim, however, a reader should refer to the text of the patent to interpret the claims. Final interpretation of a claim should be made by a patent lawyer, but an engineer or entrepreneur can often form a tentative judgment by a careful reading of his own. The following claims are used as examples in presenting typical questions of interpretation.

Examples of Method Claims

1. A method for preparing a homogeneously dispersed, unified, stable, non-phasing moldable composition of finely-divided carbon black and polymer selected from the group consisting of solid homopolymers of ethylene, solid homopolymers of propylene, solid copolymers of ethylene and propylene, and mixtures thereof, comprising providing a constantly agitated thin solution of no more than 25 percent by weight of the polymer in a solvent at a temperature above the gel point, maintaining stirring while adding 1 to 60 percent of carbon black by weight of the polymer until dispersed, cooling the mixture to its gel point while maintaining stirring and removing the solvent.

Molding Plastic (Zomlefer, U.S. 2,952,656)

This claim is "broad." It includes a wide variety of polymers and varying amounts of carbon black. However, it could be avoided (not infringed upon) by a method that used a butadiene polymer.

2. A method for improving color discrimination in a person deficient in color discrimination comprising the step of applying to one eye only a thin corneal contact lens transmitting light substantially only in the red zone and having between approximately 14 and 40 percent light transmission and substantially no transmission below approximately 590 millimicrons, the other eye being left uncovered except for the optional use of a spectacle lens, conventional corneal contact lens, or a combination thereof to provide a desired refractive correction for that eye.

Lens for Color Blind (Zeltzer, U.S. 3,586,423)

This claim would not be infringed by the use of a lens having transmission of 500 millimicrons but would be infringed if all the transmission were 620 millimicrons.

3. A process for installing wall paper on a wall comprising providing wall paper having a back portion containing dispersed permanently magnetized particles wherein a substantial component of the magnetic field lines produced by the

poles of the particles enter and leave the back surface of the wall paper in a perpendicular direction providing the wall surface with a coating of ferromagnetic, magnetically soft material, and then placing the wall paper on the wall.

Magnetic Wall Paper (Koritz, U.S. 3,235,427)

A company that manufactured and sold the magnetized wallpaper called for in this claim would be guilty of infringement even though the company did not itself carry out the process.

4. A process for applying a copper layer to a previously sensitized and super-sensitized surface comprising contacting the surface with an alkaline aqueous solution comprising copper gluconate and copper reducing agent.

Copperizing (Wein, U.S. 3,093,509)

This is an example of a "narrow" method, limited specifically to copper gluconate. Another salt of copper would not infringe on this patent.

Examples of Machine Claims

1. The combination of a tractor with a fifth-wheel assembly, a trailer having a body with a rear-end wheel assembly and with alignment and contact elements on the front end, a connecting frame having a horizontal neck, and depending vertical arms fastened together by crossbeams and connected by said fifth wheel assembly to the rear end of said tractor, a trailer elevator comprising two-way power jacks with casings connected in tandem slidably attached to the crossbeams connecting the vertical arms of said frame, means connected to said tractor for supporting and holding said horizontal neck in a substantially horizontal position during elevator operation, complementary means attached to said slidable elevator for engaging said contact elements on said trailer, hook means for locking said complementary means to said contact elements and oscillating yoke means for supporting said front end of said trailer.

Self-Raising Trailer (Tracey, U.S. 2,934,230)

This is an example of a commercially successful "narrow" claim with many elements.

2. In a sonic flow meter, an oscillator providing a continuous wave train, a modulator connected to both said oscillator and a pulse generator so as to provide pulsed wave trains, two separate identical power amplifier means connected in parallel to the output of said modulator, a separate identical transformer having its primary winding connected to the secondary winding of each transformer, said transducers being adapted to be sonically coupled to a fluid and spaced apart along the line of flow of the fluid to form a single sonic path, and phase comparing means connected between both said transducers and metering means; said pulse generator being connected across one of said transducers and arranged so as to fire the modulator only when two sonic pulses are received by the transducer after one has been emitted.

Sonic Flow Meter (Katzenstein et al., U.S. 2,991,650)

This is a "broad" claim with many elements.

3. In an electronic computing system a multiplicity of pulse responsive units constructed to receive numbers pulses having numerical significance and to receive control pulses having definite control characteristics, means to transmit to said units control pulses and numbers pulses in a correlated order including means to establish a selective relation between certain control pulses and certain predetermined units, said units being constructed for arithmetic operations and including means responsive to terminal arithmetic operation therein to transmit a control pulse effective on predetermined units for intercommunication of numerical content between one and another of said units.

Electronic Computer (Eckert and Mauchly, U.S. 3,120,606)

This is one of the main claims in Sperry-Rand's basic computer patent. It is extremely broad in scope.

Internal Protection Procedures

Patents are issued in the United States to individuals, not to companies, although legislation to change this has been proposed. Thus, a company is well advised to enter into a written agreement with all technical personnel, in which the employee grants all patent rights for his inventions to the company. Such an agreement should be drawn up by your patent lawyer to fit the circumstances of your company. Exhibit 1 contains an example of an employee agreement covering both inventions and trade secrets. (See exhibits at end of chapter.)

As noted earlier, it is important to have proof of invention. Adequate detailed and dated written records and drawings should be kept for all research and development work. Any models should be labeled and dated. All such records should bear the signatures of all witnesses to any tests or demonstrations through all experimental stages. These witnesses may someday be needed to corroborate the dates of "reduction to practice"—that is, the first successful testing of an invention.

Employees should be encouraged to use Invention Disclosure forms (Exhibit 2) to disclose all their inventions.

External Protection Procedures

Under the patent laws of most countries (but not the United States or Canada), commercial, or public, use of an invention by the inventor in that country, prior to filing a patent application in that country, nullifies his right to a patent. In the United States there is a one-year grace period; in Canada, a two-year grace period. In many foreign countries a patent right is nullified by prior public use in *any* country. In some countries, any prior publication or patent in any country, even without public use, can bar a patent (although there may be specified grace periods).

The term *public use,* as defined by the courts, often causes confusion. It is clear that ordinary sales of a production run constitute public use. In some cases, even the testing of a prototype in a customer's factory has been called a public use, in spite of evidence that the testing was purely experimental. Offering a product for sale, even though it has not yet been manufactured, has been held equivalent to public use in some cases.

In view of the differing patent regulations among the countries of the world and different interpretations of "public use," inventors should make no disclosure whatsoever to any person outside the company until a patent application is filed. In addition, the invention should not be tested outside the company, exhibited, or sold until the application is filed. Even then it may be desirable to limit the information that is published, to prevent premature disclosure of proprietary information or trade secrets. (Remember that a patent is not always granted by the Patent Office. In that event, you may have to rely on trade secret agreements.) Once a patent application has been filed in the United States, the company has one year in which to file for a patent in any foreign country. If that rule is followed, foreign countries will consider the filing effective as of the filing date in the United States.

Before discussing an invention with a potential investor—after the patent application has been filed, but perhaps before a patent has been issued, or before the details of the invention are known to the public—it is advisable to negotiate a nondisclosure agreement. This should make it clear that the potential investor will not disclose or use the invention if he does not enter into any financial relationship with the company. Such agreements, although relatively brief, are inherently complex and should be drafted for the specific occasion by the company's regular lawyer or a patent lawyer.

If you plan to offer your invention to a company other than your own, there is one danger that you should avoid. Many large companies require an inventor to sign a *non*confidential-disclosure agreement before they will consider his invention.

Such agreements usually relieve the company of any liability and are contrary to ethical business practices.

Trademarks

Your new product may or may not merit a patent, but it can always have a trademark. If you create a distinctive term, phrase, or design—one that is not confusingly similar to someone else's mark for a similar product—you may be able to register it as your trademark. Normally, the first step is to have your patent lawyer determine whether any similar mark has been registered or applied for in the U.S. Patent Office. This will usually indicate its availability and also whether or not you are infringing on someone else's mark. Upon occasion you may find that someone else has used the same mark in an area geographically remote from your company without registering it. It is therefore a good idea to follow the Patent Office search with a check of new and old trade directories, trade magazines, and telephone directories.

If your proposed trademark does not duplicate marks in the Patent Office or in trade publications, as determined in a legal opinion by your patent attorney, you can begin using the mark and instruct him to apply for a registration. If there are no complications—such as an opposition proceeding filed by a competitor—the registration may be completed within approximately one year. Once the registration has been granted, it is renewable at 20-year intervals, provided that the mark is still in use. If no one contests your mark within five years after registration, you can file an application to have your right made incontestable. A trademark may be registered for a service as well as a product, although the Patent Office sometimes rejects such marks as being merely trade names. Persistent efforts from the patent bar are making it easier to register such marks, however.

Once a trademark or service mark has been registered, you are entitled to use the legend R or "registered Trademark" on all your labeling and advertising. This marking entitles you to collect damages from an infringer even if the infringer does not have actual notice of your registration. If you sell your goods in foreign countries, you can protect your trademark by registration procedures in those countries, similar to procedures in the United States. There is one clear difference in most foreign trademark laws: the first to *register* it owns the mark. In the United States, Canada, and England, the first to *use* it owns the mark.

Copyrights–for Authors, Composers, and Artists

A trademark can be registered indefinitely. A U.S. patent lasts for 17 years. A U.S. copyright (which *cannot* be used in place of a patent) gives protection for 56 years.

A copyright is created by publishing an original work with the proper copyright notice: "© 1973 by John Sebastian." The copyright can then be recorded in the Copyright Office of the Library of Congress. The term *work* is defined by law (Title 17 of the U.S. Code) to include printed publications, books, music, maps, works of art, and motion pictures. The copyright does not protect ideas or technical information as such but protects only the mode of expression or representation. Thus no one may copy the specific form of any copyrighted program instructions, or advertisements, or illustrations. However, your competitor may use the substance of your thoughts in creating his own form of program instructions, advertisements, or illustrations.

It should be noted that U.S. copyright laws are in the process of revision at this writing. It is generally believed that the revision will extend the copyright law to all forms of information storage—for example, magnetic tapes, cores, films, and disk records. (At this time, the form of expression in a phonograph record is copyrightable apart from the music itself.) Also, the term of copyright may be extended to the life of the author plus 50 years, as is already the case in Europe.

Design Patents

Novel ornamental objects can be protected, with respect to their appearance, by what are known as "design patents." These can be applied to chairs, buildings, electrical appliances, instruments, toys, bottles, and so forth. The scope of such protection is rather narrow, however, and sometimes overlaps copyright protection. Thus an original sculpture made into a lamp base might qualify for a design patent or for a copyright. There have been several attempts made to change the law to give a single type of protection for all creative works for which style, ornamentation, and appearance are the predominant factors. These efforts have been opposed primarily by members of the garment industry, who wish to be able to copy new fashions with impunity.

Legal and Other Fees for Patents

A patent attorney is called upon to render a wide variety of services, and it is impossible to predict the fees for a particular company. An estimate can often be made for such specific matters as a preliminary patentability search, which usually costs a minimum of $150 to $200. If the search is complex, however, the cost will be substantially higher. The initial preparation and filing of a patent application will vary widely according to the subject matter and complexity. It may cost $700 or much more, but it can be estimated. The filing fee with the U.S. Patent Office, plus the fee for assigning the patent to a particular corporation, is about $100. It is difficult to predict the length of patent proceedings or to foresee the possibility of an appeal. It has been estimated that a small new company with a single principal product can expect to spend, during the first few years of its operations, approximately $5000 a year on patent matters. This amount will be much higher if the product is highly complex or if there is a contest of priority with another company. Trademark protection, on the other hand, is usually obtained for a nominal cost.

Licensing of Patents and Trademarks

A patent license is a contract in which the owner of the patent, known as the licensor, grants certain rights to another company, known as the licensee. An exclusive license is one which specifies that only the licensee may make, use, or sell the patented invention. A nonexclusive license is one that specifies that the licensee is only one of a number of companies permitted to make, use, or sell the patented product. The terms of most patent license agreements cover a wide variety of subjects. Negotiations usually include the royalty, the length of time the agreement is in force, the method of payment, penalties for violations, rights to sublicense, and an accurate description or designation of the licensed subject matter. License arrangements may be made for products with patent applications pending as well as those with issued patents. Agreements may include trade secret and know-how provisions.

Trademarks, too, can be licensed, but on a different basis. The trademark cannot be licensed itself: it must be part of a business wherein the quality of the goods meet standards designated by the licensor. Thus, a soft drink bottler who buys his syrup from the owner of the trademark and agrees to use the syrup properly in his bottling operation is, in effect, a trademark licensee.

During the past few years, both patent license agreements and trademark license agreements have been subjected to severe court rebuke when the contracts included provisions that violated the antitrust laws. License agreements cannot provide for price-fixing or for discrimination within the same class of licensees. And although licenses may be granted to only one company in a given territory, the licensee cannot be forbidden to sell outside his territory. Furthermore, license agreements have been held invalid when they have included provisions that require the licensee to purchase his requirements for nonpatented, associated articles from the licensor. Restrictions notwithstanding, a properly developed licensing program can be an important source of revenue for the owner of a patent or trademark.

Patent Suits

A lawsuit is usually the last step in a bitter dispute that cannot be resolved in any other way. It is costly and consumes valuable time and energy for the principals in the companies involved. No one should initiate litigation without a thorough review of all possible alternatives. In any lawsuit, the person initiating the suit, known as the plaintiff, is usually seeking damages or an injunction because he believes he has been wronged. If the suit is lost, the plaintiff's loss will usually be confined to his own legal expenses. The defendant in a lawsuit stands to lose much more. Not only is he forced into litigation, but he may also be forced to pay damages as well as his own legal expenses.

There are two types of patent suits. One is a suit for patent infringement, which is normally tried in a federal court. The second type of patent suit involves a licensor and a licensee. This type of suit is governed by state law and may be heard in a state or federal court. A patent owner may sue the customer of an infringer as well as the infringer himself. Thus the decision on where to bring suit may be complicated. In some cases, the loser in a patent infringement suit is ordered to pay the legal expenses of his opponent. It is important for every patent owner to mark his products with his patent number as soon as the patent is issued, in order to preserve his rights. This will have a bearing on the amount of damages awarded in a patent infringement suit. The measure of damages for patent infringement is roughly the equivalent of a reasonable royalty.

Changes in the Patent Law

At the time this chapter is being written, Congress is considering a general revision of the patent laws. One proposal under consideration would allow either the inventor or the owner of the invention to file a patent application. Another proposal would permit the publication of a pending application prior to its issuance, at the request of the applicant. Another proposal would allow any person, within six months after a patent has been issued, to notify the Patent Office that he believes the patent is invalid. If the Patent Office finds his reasons sufficient, it may reopen patent proceedings. Special provisions are also being considered for patent applications involving new microorganisms. Another significant proposal would change the term of a patent to 20 years from the date of filing rather than 17 years from the date of issue. The intent of this provision is to discourage long proceedings in the Patent Office, proceedings that can delay the issue of the patent for many years. Sperry-Rand's basic electronic computer patent, for example, was filed in 1947 but did not issue until 1964 and does not expire until 1981. Other changes, in trade secret law particularly, are occurring at frequent intervals as new court decisions are passed down.

178 Joseph Zallen

Exhibit 1

EMPLOYEE AGREEMENT RELATING TO INVENTIONS, PATENTS, AND CONFIDENTIAL INFORMATION

In consideration of my employment by the Corporation (which herein embraces _____ Corporation and its subsidiaries), and of the further continuation of such employment, and of the salary or wages paid to me in connection with such employment, and in further consideration of the sum of One Dollar paid to me by the Corporation, the receipt whereof is hereby acknowledged, and for other good and valuable consideration I agree as follows:

1. I will communicate to the Corporation promptly and fully all inventions made or conceived by me (either solely or jointly with others) during my employment, which are along the lines of the business, work, or investigations of the Corporation or which result from any work I may do for the Corporation; and such inventions, whether or not patented, shall be and remain the sole and exclusive property of the Corporation or its nominees.

2. I will keep and maintain adequate and current written records of all such inventions at all stages thereof, in the form of notes, sketches, drawings, and reports relating thereto, which records shall be and remain the property of and available to the Corporation at all times.

3. I will during and after my employment, without charge to the Corporation, but at its request and expense, assist the Corporation and its nominees in every proper way to obtain, and to vest in it or them title to, patents on such inventions in all countries, by executing all necessary or desirable documents including applications for patents and assignments thereof.

4. Unless authorized in writing, or instructed, by the Corporation, I will not during or after my employment disclose to

others, or use, any of the Corporation's secret or confidential information, knowledge or data relating thereto unless and until, and then to the extent and only to the extent that such information, knowledge or data becomes available to the public otherwise than by my act or omission.

5. I warrant that I have not previously assumed any obligations inconsistent with those of this agreement.

6. This agreement shall be binding on my heirs, legal representatives and assigns, and shall inure to the benefit of any successors and assigns of the Corporation.

7. This agreement supersedes all previous agreements, written or oral, relating to the above subject matter, and shall not be changed orally.

8. This agreement shall be construed according to the laws of the State of _____, U.S.A.

_____

(Employee's Signature, including full first name)

ACCEPTED AND AGREED TO:

THE CORPORATION   Witness:

By _____   _____

Date: _____   Date: _____

Exhibit 2

INSTRUCTIONS FOR
INVENTION DISCLOSURE FORM

This form is provided for your assistance in the submission of ideas and discoveries and is intended to benefit both you and the _____ Company. Do not hesitate to submit any idea in any way new as far as your knowledge goes. Supporting data is desirable but not essential. Do not prejudge the patentability of any idea or discovery.

"Title of Invention" should embrace a concise but descriptive title from which the general subject matter can readily be gathered. Include all participants without attempting to determine inventorship.

Under "Prior Art Background" and "Advantages of Proposal" the inventor should set forth generally any information he has regarding what was known and done heretofore in the same and related fields and how this failed to solve the problem satisfactorialy. The inventor should then state wherein his proposal does solve the problem and what advantages it provides over the prior art.

In the "Detailed Description" the disclosure should err on the side of more rather than less description. This should point up the special features or distinguishing characteristics of the invention, include such data as is available to illustrate the emphasized features, stress anything of a critical nature in proportions or dimensions and, in the case of any compounds or new processes involving the use of specific materials, should indicate what, if any, other materials are regarded by the inventor as equivalents. Any other information as to the origin of, or inspiration for, the invention which is not mentioned under "Prior Art Background" and "Advantages of Proposal" should be set forth here.

It is desirable to include, preferably at the end of the "Detailed Description", a statement as to availability of notebooks and laboratory or plant records.

Each page of this invention disclosure should preferably be dated and signed by the inventor or inventors, and also by at least one and preferably two witnesses who understand the proposal.

INVENTION DISCLOSURE FORM

Date_____
Dept._____
From_____

1. *Title of Invention*

_____
_____
_____
_____

2. *Names and Addresses of all Possible Inventors*

_____
_____
_____
_____

3. *Prior Art Background*

_____
_____
_____
_____
_____
_____
_____
_____
_____

4. *Advantages of Proposal*

_____
_____
_____
_____
_____
_____

5. *Detailed Description* (*including attached sketches*)

_____

_____

_____

_____

_____

_____

_____

_____

_____

_____

_____

                    (Signed)_____

                              _____

Disclosure explained to
and understood by:
        Name_____   Date_____

                    Address_____

        Name_____   Date_____

                    Address_____

IV BUSINESS STRATEGY AND DEVELOPMENT

As a new entrepreneur who has just been funded with his initial money, you will find yourself faced with a difficult choice: Should you risk everything to achieve exponential growth by expensive advertising and high-volume production to achieve low cost, or should you take a more conservative approach and grow more slowly? The first strategy has sometimes been called "You bet your company," or as Bruce Backe has indicated, it is a strategy of "Go for broke" or "Go broke." Whenever a new entrepreneur achieves great success, there is a general feeling that the "You bet your company" approach was the strategy he followed. As an entrepreneur, you have already established yourself as a risk taker, and there is a great tendency to continue that philosophy into your business policies.

One theme in the advice that the following chapters put forward is not to pursue the "You bet your company" approach. For example, when you develop a new product, have a customer share the cost with you. When you introduce a new product and develop the promotional material, take advantage of all the free publicity available before paying for promotion. When you develop your production capability, buy your parts in small quantities with provision for a rake-back on price as your volume increases. All of these approaches, which are suggested in the chapters to follow, recognize the fact that as a new entrepreneur you may be relatively inexperienced in running your own business. Therefore you should move your company at a moderate pace in the beginning until you learn what you are about. Think of your growth as a two-stage process. The first stage is one in which you establish yourself as an entrepreneur and avoid going bankrupt. The second stage is one in which you establish yourself as a successful businessman and the stock of your company as a growth investment.

Every enterprise has a basic strategy or way of doing business, whether articulated or not, which it hopes and believes will enable it to succeed. Often this strategy is arrived at intuitively, never stated explicitly, and sometimes not even recognized by those who are following it. The implementation of the basic business strategy includes but is not limited to the following areas, each of which has its own strategy:

1. Defining the market
2. Product development
3. Distribution (sales)
4. Promotion
5. Pricing
6. Production
7. Financial controls

Strategy Development*

True strategic victories are won by using corporate resources to substantially outperform a competitor with superior strength. The concept of superior performance without superior resources is usually identified with trying harder. Yet most companies seem to work very hard to produce only minor differentials in performance.

* This brief discussion on business strategy concepts is abstracted from the *Perspectives* series by Bruce Henderson, published by the Boston Consulting Group, Inc.

The underlying principle of good strategy is simple: "Concentrate your strength against your competitor's relative weakness." This principle has a major corollary in a dynamic competitive environment: Concentration of effort will inevitably produce a counterconcentration by the competition; therefore timing and sequence are critical. A major attack should never be launched against a competent, well-entrenched competitor without first eliminating his ability or willingness to respond in kind.

There are many prerequisites to a successful strategy:

- The characteristics of the competition must be known in detail, including their characteristic attitudes and behavior.
- The environment in which competition will take place must be equally well understood.
- Your own relative strengths must be accurately and objectively appraised.
- The strategic concept must not be based on the obvious exercise of known strengths. If it is, you don't need a strategy; you just need a plan.
- It must be possible to achieve stability if the strategy succeeds.
- Your own organization must not be misled by your efforts to outmaneuver competition. Strategic goals must be very explicit.

Once the strategic framework has been designed, the tactics of attack must be selected. Concentration of resources can be achieved in several ways:

- Choose the most vulnerable market segment.
- Choose products or markets that require response rates beyond a competitor's ability.
- Choose products or markets requiring capital that a competitor is unwilling to commit.
- Recognize the commercial potentials of new technology early.

- Exploit managerial differences in style, method, or system such as overhead rate, distribution channels, market image, or flexibility.

The value of the initiative depends on when and how the competition responds. Therefore an effective strategy must choose the best initiative and must dissuade the competition from responding. This is a fundamental strategic concept that is often neglected. Most strategic success depends upon the competition's decision not to compete. Consequently success almost always depends upon the ability to influence a competitor's decisions. It is necessary to win in the mind of the competition.

Diversion and dissuasion fall into classic categories:

- *Appear to be unworthy of attention.* Quickly cut off a part of the market that is too small to justify a major response. Repeat this tactic over and over.
- *Appear to be unbeatable.* Convince competitors that if they follow your lead and practices, they will gain nothing since you will equal or better any market actions they take.
- *Avoid attention.* Be secretive. Do not let the competition know about new products, new policies, or new capabilities until it is too late to respond effectively.
- *Redirect attention.* Focus competitors' attention on the major volume areas of company sales, not on the high-potential areas.
- *Attract attention but discredit significance.* Overstate and overpublicize the potentials of new products or policies.
- *Be apparently irrational.* Take actions that seem emotional or impulsive but that make competitive investment unattractive.

What you may gain from these remaining chapters is a better insight into how to spend your dollars wisely. Parkinson's Law applies not only to large bureaucracies but to your company as well. Time and dollars are the crucial elements. As you let items slip for a day or two, those days turn into weeks and the weeks into months and the end of the year into bankruptcy. Every one hundred dollars or fifty dollars that you decide is not important will soon accumulate to a thousand dollars, and a thousand dollars is important. You should be prepared to scrap for every dollar and every day. The entrepreneur's motto is "Do tonight what you can do tomorrow."

One of your more important activities will be the preparation of budgeted cash flow forecasts. Everyone is familiar with the saying "The fool and his money are soon parted." Venture capitalists know that an engineer and his money are also soon parted. Therefore, as you approach the end of this book, you should realize that within every new company there must be some hard-nosed fellow who acts as the conservative lever in the company, ensuring that those budgets are met and that, when they are not, corrective actions are taken quickly, before serious cash flow problems set in.

This book ends with a chapter on consulting. It is included here because so many new ventures begin as consulting partnerships that later initiate or are transformed into product businesses. While much of what has been said in previous chapters applies to consulting, some of the special considerations that are unique to consulting are discussed in this chapter.

William D. Putt
Kenneth J. Germeshausen

11 MARKET STRATEGY
Arthur P. Alexander*

There seem to be two ways of doing things: the "hard way" and the "easy way." In starting a new business enterprise, the hard and easy ways are dependent upon the amount of money available. Certain tasks are a lot easier to perform and certain goals are more attainable with adequate financing. There are many entrepreneurial start-up situations that can be cited where financing is not a problem; however, more often than not, money is not available in quantities necessary to do the job "properly." This chapter is written with the assumption (probably quite correct) that there is inadequate financing to do everything "first class"; thus lack of necessary funds makes the job of getting goods and services to the market at a profit much more difficult. How can the job be done? Where do you start?

I shall try to develop some insight into the development of a market strategy by relating my own experience in three different areas:

• Market analysis
• Product development and merchandising
• Pricing

* Arthur P. Alexander received his A.B. degree from Boston University and his S.B. in management from M.I.T. He was founder and president of Allaco Products, Inc., and is currently president of A.P.I., Inc.

Market Analysis

In 1962 my partner and I started our company with a total
initial capitalization of $25. At the beginning we had no plant
or equipment and no technical expertise in our particular field,
the formulation of industrial chemicals.

We took ease of entry as one of our fundamental criteria for
selecting a product area. Ease of entry was evaluated from
every aspect: capital investment, technology, competition,
plant and equipment requirements, product development,
product line, sales effort, delay time in making the first sale,
simplicity in application and use, channels of distribution,
pricing, location of market, and so forth. On the basis of all of
these inputs we decided that a line of adhesives would be our
most successful product area.

Our method of acquiring the information necessary to make
this decision involved contacting several potential customers to
explain our plans to enter the industrial adhesive field. We
asked the following questions: What did they think of the idea?
Was there room for another formulator? Did they have any
thoughts on the future of the products we would be formu-
lating? Would they buy from us? How much material would
they use? How much would they pay? What were they using at
that time? What were they looking for in a supplier, products,
price and service? Following the feedback we obtained from
the customers, we contacted next the raw material suppliers.
We obtained from them additional valuable information.
These suppliers gave us an insight on the following important
points:

1. How much and what type of plant and equipment are
   necessary for the manufacture of the different product lines?
   This information told us what industry we should enter first.

2. What is the basic formulation for each product line?
3. What special technology is required for each product line?
4. What industry is the easiest to penetrate, and why?

Product Development and Merchandising

On the basis of the information we gathered in our market analysis, we decided that industrial adhesives could be sold most effectively through direct salesmen in a small, clearly defined geographic area, New England. Even though products in this classification were being sold at the time in New England by other suppliers, the market had not been developed to its full potential. We found that the competition was selling through sales representatives, thus considerably weakening its sales and market development.

Manufacturing the product line was our next problem. Remember, we had no plant and equipment or money to invest in manufacturing. The raw material supplier told us that the type of equipment used to formulate our products was also used in several other noncompetitive industries. Thus we located a company that had the necessary equipment and available equipment time (nights and weekends) and was willing to subcontract the manufacture of our product line. A complete line included approximately twelve products. But rather than initially manufacturing all these items, we decided that five basic products would be adequate. It is interesting to note that ten years later we still distribute this particular line of products by direct sales in the initial New England marketing area, and we are the leading supplier in the field. It should also be pointed out that the product has not done well in other parts of the country where it was sold through manufacturer's representatives and distributors.

Pricing

How is the price set for a new product? This shouldn't be very difficult to do because there is usually more than enough information available. These are the things to check:

1. What is the product competing against?
2. What are the total manufacturing costs?
3. What profit margin is desired?
4. What are the representatives' commissions or distributors' discounts involved?

In our initial product line, we decided to price as high as the highest competitor's price. We justified this position by being able to offer something to the customer which he was not getting at the time from the existing suppliers—service. In a word, we were being more responsive to the customer's needs. This pricing technique was so successful over the years that it became yet another facet of our corporate image—high prices. This was probably the single most important factor in shaping the format and image of our company. In effect, we said, "We will operate under the philosophy of low volume–high margin." This is not a bad philosophy for a small company starting out. We have had many situations where the high price of an established product was a deterrent to volume business. In these cases, if possible, the product was modified, renamed, and sold as a speciality item to a single customer at a reduced price. Thus, by staying with a high-price policy, we could always lower the price to a single customer for volume usage. That is to say, it was not a published price. It is always easier to lower the price than to raise it.

In recent years, with more plant and equipment available, we have solicited business that would be considered high volume–low margin. We have amalgamated both philosophies quite successfully without detriment to our established image. The reason for this success is that our customers know that just because the product has a lower price tag it does not mean that it is inferior. It means that it has a more limited use. We found that if a less expensive product is not oversold, that is, if the product is not recommended for an application beyond its performance capabilities, then we have no problem.

In retrospect, I should point out that we made a mistake by not going after the high-volume, low-profit business. We should have entered this end of the pricing spectrum several years earlier than we did. We were quite satisfied with our margin business; had we entered this high-volume market earlier, we would have had faster growth sooner. We later proved that we could indeed go after both ends of the price range quite successfully.

In conclusion, this process of determining what the market will bear is a difficult one, especially if approached from the point of view of charging higher prices and working down. For a new company it is a risky strategy because there may not be sufficient funds to make the second and third attempts. Competition is tough, and whoever said that competition was good probably worked for a public utility. Unless you are selling ads for the Yellow Pages in the Soviet Union, you had better be prepared to consider price as a key element. And the time to consider price in the development of your market strategy is before the product has been designed, not after. The fait accompli is death for the small company in the pricing area.

12 PACKAGING, DISTRIBUTION, AND PROMOTION
F. Douglas Van Sicklen*

Closing a sale is the ultimate goal for the entrepreneur. Successful selling includes all those activities that induce the customer to place his order. In this chapter I shall discuss packaging, distribution, and promotion—all part of the selling effort.†

Packaging

In its broadest sense, "packaging" includes a product's appearance, its aesthetic appeal, as well as its wrapping for shipment or display in a store or other outlet. Even after a product has been conceived, designed, prototyped, and engineered for manufacturing, it may not be ready for the market. The next stage of its development is in the area of industrial design: how it looks not only at the point of sale but when in use. Acceptance in the marketplace does involve a product's appearance as well as its usefulness. No matter how many people tell you that no one cares what a product looks like as long as it works, the fact is that if it doesn't look right, the

---

* F. Douglas Van Sicklen received his S.B. degree from M.I.T. and his M.B.A. from the Harvard Business School. He had a distinguished career with several large corporations and then became president of XYZ Corporation. He is currently chairman of Western Metal Industries Corporation.
† All dollar figures in this chapter are in 1972 dollars.

customer won't even turn on the switch to see if it works.

What decisions are involved in packaging? Typical questions concern your product's optimum size, shape, and color. Some of these aspects of its design will be determined by the competition, the field of technology, the price, and the market. For example, if your product is test equipment for a production line, perhaps you should make it easy to move from place to place, on a caddie cart with wheels or a shoulder strap. Does it have to be stored at night or when not in use? Perhaps it needs a protective cover. Should that be metal or plastic? What does the competition's product look like? Do competitive devices all look alike? Do they have to look alike? Can the product's encasement be made functional as well as decorative? Where in the customer's environment will the product be used: office, shop, showroom, factory, or home; bedroom, kitchen, or cellar; floor or desk? Where will it be when in use and when not in use?

A well-known electronics company manufactures a product used in the navigation of small yachts. Technically, there is nothing better on the market. But in a small pitching, rolling boat the device constantly falls over. It is unstable in a seaway. The company has added a small steel plate to stabilize the device, but it is obviously an afterthought and has not solved the problem. A large number of sales are being lost, not because of poor performance or unattractive appearance, but because the manufacturer did not take into account the conditions under which the product would be used. The only solution, despite the cost, is a totally new design.

The services of a good industrial designer are sometimes invaluable in packaging a new product. An outside designer, someone not emotionally involved with the product, may make an enormous contribution to the product's market appeal. You should talk to several designers, get cost estimates, look at samples of their work, and check their references thoroughly. An industrial design job will cost $2000 or more and should include schematic drawings, artistic renderings, engineering drawings, and manufacturing drawings. In addition to the design of the product itself, the project might include the outer wrappings (for example, a permanent carrying case or a disposable cardboard box), instruction and warranty slips, individual shipping cartons, and en route advertising (printing on the outside of cartons). If you are in a highly competitive field, your designer should attempt to create a look that will distinguish your product from its competitors.

Some designers specialize in consumer products, some in complex technical products, some in basic industrial products. Most will tell you that they design anything that has to be sold, but if you look at their portfolios, you will find that each designer tends to do better in a specific area of design—for example, the corporate logo (trademarks or symbols) or illustrations for instruction manuals. Study the field carefully before you make your choice.

It is a good idea to have your corporate logo and packing materials designed at the same time as your product. An integrated design package will enhance your corporate image. You can't judge a book by its cover, but a good cover sells a lot of books. This applies to your company's image as well as its products.

Let's look at an example. In the 1960s, our company introduced a new product to the marketplace, a small digital computer encased in a black metal box about the size and shape of a cigar box. On the front of the box were several knobs and dials. When these were set in certain positions and the "start" switch was activated, the box played a single-noted tune. Its inventor called it "The Music Box," to suggest a small Swiss music box that is wound up to play a tune. Our "music box" ran on batteries and could be programmed to play a tune that would never repeat itself in 30 years of playing time. We took the prototype out on the road: to Jordan Marsh, Lechmere Sales, and Shreve, Crump, & Low in Boston; to The Emporium in San Francisco; to Macy's, Bernard Altman's, and Abercrombie & Fitch in New York City; and to many other stores in cities across the country. It was a consumer product, so we talked to store owners, buyers, salespeople, and customers. We asked a lot of questions. What do you think of it? What should it look like? What department would you sell it in? How much should it sell for? Who will buy it? How should we advertise it? We gathered thousands of suggestions, hired an industrial designer (after interviewing and investigating several), and redesigned "The Music Box."

We thought it would appeal to the younger generation; so very deliberately we selected a design that completely changed its image. We renamed it "The Muse" and priced it at $300. Within five months we had received over $1,700,000 in orders. It has won numerous design awards and is on permanent display in the Museum of Science and the Museum of Fine Arts in Boston. We added an integrated "psychedelic" light show ($180 retail) and a speaker-amplifier ($180 retail) and attached electric cords so that it could be plugged into a wall socket. In all, four and one-half months elapsed between the building of a prototype of "The Music Box" and the manufacturing of "The Muse." The manufacturing cost was less than $100 a unit, subcontracted. The design cost was $8000, including an outer casing and shipping cartons. The designer in this instance made a major contribution to the success of the product. In its original state, "The Music Box" was an intriguing device. Redesigned, "The Muse" was an outstanding marketing success.

Distribution

Who is going to sell your product? Since you know more about it than anyone else, you may be the best salesman. In any event, you should try to sell at least a few units yourself to get a feel for the market. The experience will help you in your choice of future salesmen: you will know what they are likely to be up against. As your company grows, you will have to consider the value of a direct sales force as opposed to distributors and manufacturers' representatives. A salesman works solely for you, and the sales he makes must be sufficient to cover his salary. A distributor usually stocks your product along with others. He may be required to take a minimum order, in return for which he will receive a large discount on list price (30–60 percent). When he buys the product outright (that is, not on consignment), he can resell it at any price he chooses. A manufacturers' representative works on commission only. He sells products for many manufacturers and is paid when goods are shipped or when they are paid for. His commission may range from 2 to 12 percent. He pays his own expenses and furnishes his own car and gas. You provide him with free product literature and demonstration models.

Salesmen, distributors, and manufacturers' representatives eventually all reach the same customer. Your own salesman depends completely on your product for his success and may work harder. On the other hand, he is expensive. No matter how meager his salary, he gets paid once a month, plus all expenses, whether or not he makes sales. There are several advantages to using a distributor instead. He does not get paid, and he has products ready for immediate delivery to the customer. If his money is invested in your product, he must sell it as rapidly as possible to make a profit. He may also give you sizable orders at regular intervals. It is more likely, however, that he will take your product on consignment only, until he is sure it will sell. And when he buys outright, he will take a hefty discount. A manufacturers' representative, the third alternative, is paid only for actual sales, thus minimizing your cash flow and risk. He may also provide broad geographic coverage in a short period of time. But he sells many other products and may do very little missionary sales work for a new product. If your product is technologically complex, he may make poor presentations. You will then have to spend a lot of time training him and making sure he gives your product sufficient attention.

Many companies start out with manufacturers' representatives if their product is not highly technical and can be easily demonstrated. It is customary to prepare an agreement that states in simple terms that you have both agreed that he will sell your product in a particular territory (usually the one in which he is already working), that you agree to pay a specific commission on sales, that the agreement is in effect until canceled by either party, and that it may be canceled by either party with a 30-day notice. Commission percentages will depend on the difficulty of making sales as well as the sales price itself.

How do you locate a manufacturer's representative? Study trade publications and the Yellow Pages of your telephone book. Talk to several representatives who are selling in your field, and try to persuade each one to sell your product; then choose the best one, perhaps someone who has his own office, staff, and several salesmen. You can usually judge the performance of a manufacturers' representative within 60 to 90 days. If he does not do well, dissolve your agreement and sign up someone else. But it is best not to change representatives too often, or your product will get the reputation of being no good or tough to sell. When that happens, manufacturers' representatives will not be willing to sell it at all or will demand higher commissions.

Sooner or later, most companies need at least one full-time salesman of their own. To find your first salesman, you can run a classified ad in your local paper after talking to local personnel agencies to determine the going pay scale. If this method doesn't work, you may want to read the "Positions Wanted" column in *The Wall Street Journal* or place an ad of your own. Salesmen found through this channel may be expensive, however, if you have to pay travel and moving expenses. A one-inch ad in the Eastern edition of *The Wall Street Journal* costs about $150 a day, while an ad in your local paper costs only $3–10 a day. Being frugal may lead you to some good salesmen in your own hometown.

Try to find a salesman who has handled your type of product before. He will be familiar with distribution and marketing methods and won't have to learn them on your time. If you interview as many people as possible for the job, you may learn a lot from them about the market, selling methods, and promotional techniques. Interview experienced and inexperienced people, younger and older people. My choice in a start-up situation is usually a man between the ages of twenty-five and thirty-five. If your product is a technologically sophisticated device, you may want a salesman with a college degree in your field, but you will have to pay more for such a person. A degree is not always essential, but it may indicate that the potential salesman has the capacity to develop as your company expands. A good start-up salesman will cost about $16,000 a year, plus expenses, plus a commission (about 2 percent on gross shipments a year after the first $500,000). Do not pay flat salary only, because this gives the salesman no incentive and he will be dissatisfied with this type of arrangement within a year if he is doing a good job. Make it clear that a commission is paid when shipments are made, not when orders are taken. This is a cardinal rule for manufacturers' representatives as well as salesmen. Do not offer stock or options or bonuses at first, because you don't know enough about your total sales picture yet or your business as a whole to give extra fringe benefits. If all goes well, you may want to give your salesman two weeks' salary at the end of his first year, but this should not be part of your base hiring plan.

It is customary to pay your salesman about ten cents a mile if he uses his own car. (You should not furnish a company car for the first year.) Pay travel expenses based on weekly or monthly expense reports. Check the expense reports personally to be sure of their accuracy and to keep track of your sales costs. It is best not to pinch pennies on your salesman, however. That may hurt his ego, and a salesman's ego is often extremely sensitive. But see that he keeps his expenses within reason.

Promotion

Once your product has been packaged, or designed, and the distribution system determined, you will need sales brochures, posters, and other promotional literature to help sell the product without an actual demonstration. First, prepare a preliminary price list including (1) the list, or retail, price, that is, the final price to the person who uses the product; (2) the wholesale price, that is, the price a distributor pays; and (3) quantity discounts. (You may charge a certain price for one item, a lower price per item if the customer or distributor buys between ten and 15 items; an even lower price per item if he buys between 16 and 30, and so on). If your product will compete with a product already on the market, pick up a competitor's price list from a distributor and follow that order of presentation. Your prices will thus be more realistic, and the distributor can make convenient comparisons between competing products and prices.

Promotional literature should include a picture or a sketch of your product and a picture of your manufacturing plant or place of business if the latter will enhance your corporate image. If your product has not reached its final stage of industrial design when you are preparing promotional literature, you can have a sketch made by an advertising agency for a few hundred dollars. Or an airbrush illustration may interest you. This looks like an actual photograph but costs about $3000–4000 for a 24″ × 30″ picture. The only time you should consider paying this high a price is when you must have a picture for your sales effort well in advance of production.

Armed with a two-color illustration (white plus two other colors) and a preliminary price list, you are ready to call on customers, manufacturers' representatives, wholesalers, and retailers to test their reactions to your product. This is done before setting firm prices and before trying to obtain orders. After these interviews, you can prepare your final sales brochure. Write a description of your product under its picture—your best two-minute sales pitch. It is advisable not to mention price unless price is a basic feature in the product's sales appeal. What should you call your product? I give my products names like "The Muse," "Startrek II," and "The X-45," rather than "World Technology Corporation's Multiple Optical Scanner and Photosynthesizing Processor." A brief name makes for a smoother sales presentation. Simple, straightforward price lists, illustrations, and one-page brochures are not only cheap but also best suited for the market entry of industrial products. Most buyers, purchasing agents, and engineers prefer that you omit the frills. For a consumer product, however, you may need more glamorous promotional literature. The consumer is so used to extravagant advertising that he or she may ignore a quick, simple, no-nonsense presentation.

When you are having your preliminary price sheets printed up (about 500), have some order books printed too. The printer should be able to show you samples of order books, shipping papers, and labels and help you solve any printing problems. When you have decided on your final prices, prepare a one-sheet flyer for each product, as well as an overall price list. Order about 2500 copies of each for an industrial product; about 5000 for a consumer product.

When your promotional literature is ready, it is time to begin an active selling campaign. Consider your advertising strategy first. Which of the media will you use: television, radio, space advertising (magazines and newspapers), or direct mail? Television and radio commercials are the most expensive but produce the best results for consumer products. Direct mail is the least expensive. It is a good idea to set an advertising budget before you talk to an advertising agency. Ask an agency what it can do on a specific budget; never leave the cost up in the air. In the Boston area the monthly retainer for a good advertising agency is about $1000. For this price the agency handles all advertising and publicity at cost. For "The Muse," our total advertising budget was $30,000, including all our promotional literature.

Before you get into more expensive advertising, plan a direct mail campaign with flyers, brochures, reprints of news releases, announcements of dealer appointments, testimonials, and any other publicity your product receives. Your agency can buy appropriate mailing lists for you. In figuring the expense of a direct mailing, you should include envelopes, postage, the promotional material, and the time of the personnel who collate the material.

There are other approaches to the public that you should consider as soon as possible because they are virtually free. Your advertising agency should be able to help you make contacts that will lead to free exposure. For example, you will not be charged for announcements in new-product columns in trade magazines, and these may elicit queries from readers. The only cost here is the preparation of the news release by your agency. You, or your agent, may also be able to persuade television and radio talk-show hosts to invite you on their programs to discuss your product. They are always looking for unusual ideas and inventions to present to their audiences. We were invited to appear on several such shows across the country to talk about "The Muse," thanks to the efforts of our free-lance public relations agent. She was also able to get our product into a center-page spread in *Industry Magazine* and into the gift sections of Christmas issues of *Esquire* and *Playboy*—all free.

Since our industrial designer had a stake in our success, his public relations agency also went to work on our behalf. The agency entered "The Muse" in design competitions, and when awards were announced in local and national newspapers and magazines, we gathered free publicity. After about three months of promotion, the executives of our company were invited to speak at the Tuck School of Business Administration at Dartmouth, the Wharton School of Finance and Commerce at the University of Pennsylvania, Massachusetts Institute of Technology, and Harvard University.

During all promotional campaigns, there are bound to be many discouraging moments and numerous blind alleys. Nevertheless, it is important to communicate your enthusiasm through every available channel, whether it is commercial advertising, personal contacts, or publicity appearances. You should answer every inquiry, pursue every contact, explore every lead. Someday, after months of exhausting effort, your telephone will ring, and someone who sounds as though he is calling from the bottom of a barrel will utter the long-awaited, magic words: "I want to place an order."

13 FINANCIAL CONTROLS

Ronald Pettirossi*

Many of your important decisions during start-up and later will involve financial considerations such as whether to buy or lease machinery and equipment, whether to increase the price of your product as the result of a rent hike, whether to hire a salesman or use a manufacturers' representative on commission. For any given time period, you may have to decide among competing priorities such as whether to increase research and development activity or to undertake an advertising campaign. You will have to decide when to seek financing, whether to look for private investors or to request a capital loan from an institutional source, when to make a public offering. To monitor and evaluate your company's performance and financial needs, you must have accurate and accessible financial information.

Once you have negotiated a deal and obtained your initial financing, an accurate and organized system of controls is essential. Your investors will analyze your records to determine how well you are using their money and whether or not to provide additional financing when you need it. Financial institutions will examine your records if you apply for a

* Ronald P. Pettirossi received his B.B.A. degree from the University of Massachusetts. He has been with Arthur Young & Co. since 1964, working with many small and new businesses, and is currently an audit principal with the firm in Hartford, Connecticut.

working capital loan. In fact, institutional lenders often request financial projections from potential borrowers for the purpose of determining their awareness of financial concepts, the logic of their sales and profit objectives, and the overall credibility of the company's past, present, and projected performance.

What happens to a company that does not use basic financial controls? Financial projections, growth objectives, and economic decisions based on inaccurate data almost invariably lead to financial chaos. When a company starts to make inept financial decisions, becomes financially overextended, starts to fall behind in its obligations to vendors and in production and shipping schedules, stockholders and investors rapidly lose confidence in its credibility. The entrepreneur may become desperate for further financing and be forced to accept help from any available source. But at what price? The price may be losing control of his company and becoming an employee instead of the employer. Ambitions and dreams then give way to frustration and dissatisfaction. Even if the company succeeds, investors claim most of the rewards.

Here is an example of what can happen without financial controls. One small young company based its products' selling price on estimated product cost plus a profit factor of 10 percent. Since no procedures were developed to collect data and to make meaningful cost reports by the month, the founders did not learn until the end of the year that they were actually selling their product at less than cost. The projected production learning curve never materialized. The result was that although they had realized a small profit the year before, for the current year they lost over $100,000 on sales of $700,000.

Financial controls do not guarantee that this type of situation will not develop, but they provide an absolutely essential foundation for informed decision making. The purpose of this chapter is neither to teach you accounting nor to show you how to interpret and evaluate financial data. By touching on some of the most basic components of an adequate system, however, I hope to give you a better understanding of the structure of such a system. It will then be up to you to design and implement your own system.

The Basic Records for a Financial Control System

To maintain adequate financial controls, a company must keep at least the following records:
1. Sales journal—a detailed, daily listing of sales
2. Voucher register—a detailed daily listing of liabilities and expenses incurred
3. Payroll journal—a detailed listing of employees' wages and withholdings thereon. This not only is necessary for internal accounting but is the basis for the preparation of federal, state, and local tax forms.
4. Cash receipts book—a detailed daily listing of incoming cash from all sources
5. Cash disbursements book—a detailed listing of all outgoing cash and checks. This ledger is usually maintained in addition to the information provided by the stubs of your checkbook.
6. General ledger—monthly (or more frequent) summaries of the daily activities recorded in the company accounts (above). This ledger provides the basic information for the company's financial statements.
7. General journal—a record of any financial activity not included in other journals of original entry (for example, depreciation, loan repayment, sale of stock).
The following paragraphs contain simplified illustrations of the records described above, to demonstrate the basic uses for each.
The totals of the income account (sales journal) and the

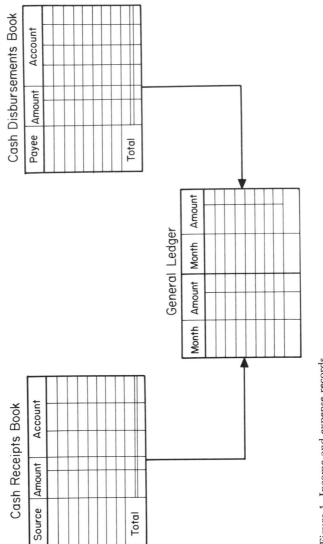

Figure 1. Income and expense records

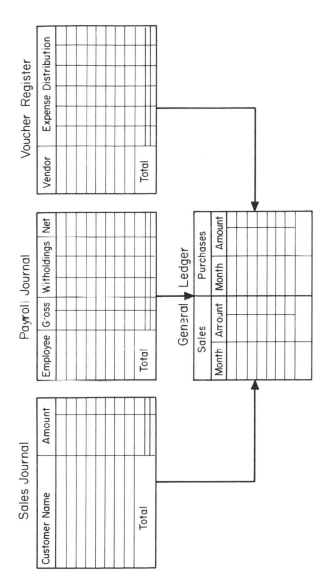

Figure 2. Records of cash activity

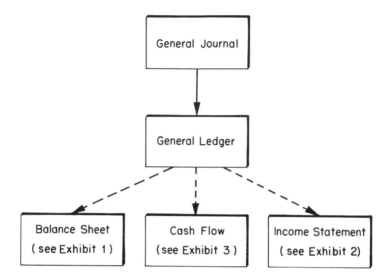

Figure 3. Financial statements

expense accounts (payroll journal and voucher register) are recorded in the general ledger periodically (usually monthly). The basic records (sales journal, payroll journal, and voucher register) and the underlying material (sales slips, purchase orders, vouchers, and so on) should be maintained by clerical personnel. The general ledger requires more skilled accounting.

The totals of cash received (cash receipts book) and cash disbursed (cash disbursement book) are also posted to the general ledger periodically (usually monthly). Basic records should be maintained (with accompanying receipts, and so on) by the company's clerical staff.

Once all activity for a month, quarter, or year has been summarized (including data in the general journal, as shown in Exhibit 2) and posted to the general ledger, the financial statements—usually a balance sheet (Exhibit 1) and an income statement (Exhibit 2)—can be prepared. Another statement that should be prepared, but which is often neglected, is the cash flow statement (Exhibit 3). This report helps the company to determine the availability of cash and to relate balance sheet figures to income statement figures. Without an adequate understanding of cash flow, a company may end up "cash poor," unable to meet its current obligations, although its balance sheet and income statement show it to be making a profit.

Balance sheets, income statements, and cash flow statements should be prepared by someone who is trained in the field of accounting. If this work is assigned to the clerical and secretarial personnel who maintain daily journals, your financial records will probably be incomplete and inaccurate. You will then have to pay a high fee at the end of the year to have an accountant or an auditing firm put your records in order for audit and tax purposes. In addition to basic clerical personnel (for whom annual salaries range from $5000 to $7000), therefore, you may want to hire a trained bookkeeper, controller, or outside accountant. The choice will depend on the size and complexity of your business. Annual salaries for a trained bookkeeper range from $8000 to $12,000; for a controller, from $12,000 to $20,000; for an outside professional, from $15 to $20 an hour.

Cash Flow

As the pace of your new business quickens, you will learn that there are two basic measures of financial success. The first is what is "below the line" (profit). This determines the value of your stock. The second is what is in the company's bank account (cash). This determines whether you will be around next month to continue your operation. Since usually you will have no profits in the beginning, efficient management of cash flow—the receipt and disbursement of funds—may mean the difference between success or failure for your company. A number of the proposals that I receive from new entrepreneurs do not include cash flow statements. Many entrepreneurs assume that their profit-and-loss statements will indicate how much cash their companies require. A few examples of cash flow problems will show the fallibility of this assumption.

1. Profit-and-loss statements include a cost called "depreciation." The purpose of depreciation is to allow a company to allocate the cost of its equipment and other fixed assets over their estimated productive life-span. If the company actually pays cash for a piece of equipment at the time of its purchase, depreciation in subsequent years will not represent a cash outflow but will merely reflect the spread of the cost over a specific, predetermined time period. For this reason, when cash flow for a particular time period is being determined from the net profit figure, the net profit must be increased by the amount of the depreciation expense included therein.

2. Another example of the need for a cash flow statement is a situation that sometimes occurs when customers stretch out their payments for purchases (usually in a "soft" economy). Although you may be selling more and therefore generating more profit, you may find that you are short of cash to pay your suppliers because your customers are paying you in installments.

3. The expiration of a loan requires repayment. This payment will never appear on your profit-and-loss statement, but it certainly means that you need cash, perhaps more than is available in the business at that time.

These examples illustrate that "profit" and "cash" are fundamentally different concepts. The basic approach for determining how much cash will be required in a particular month is to examine the profit-and-loss statement for that month and to note the changes that occur in the balance sheet at the beginning and the end of that month. Table 1 indicates how this might be done.

This example shows how a company can make a profit and at

Table 1

Profit-and-Loss Statement–January, 1974

Sales	$287.00
Costs	−245.00
	$ 42.00 (a positive cash inflow assuming no depreciation)

Balance Sheet Statement

	January 1	February 1	Net Change in Cash Position
Total assets	$2000	$2100	−$100
Total liabilities	1120	1000	−120
Common stock	137	137	0
			$220 (cash outflow)

the same time have a shortage of cash. The company's profit in January was $42, but it actually "lost" $178 in cash. This is what happened. The company's accounts receivable rose $100 for the month, raising its total assets from $2000 to $2100. This means that of the $287 worth of sales made in January, only $187 were paid for in cash. At the same time, liabilities were reduced from $1120 to $1000 as the result of paying off a loan. So in January the company received $187 in cash and made cash disbursements of $365 (costs = $245; repayment of loan = $120). Although the company's net profit was indeed $42, its cash outflow exceeded its cash inflow by $178.

Financial Projections

When you maintain records such as those described at the beginning of this chapter, you are laying the groundwork for an effective system of controls. Still it is not enough to know what has happened in the past. No control system is complete if you cannot anticipate future performance. In addition to reporting current transactions, you should prepare a monthly set of financial projections. (See Exhibit 1.) These forecasts should use the same cost categories and be prepared in the same detail as your current financial reports. This will make it possible for you to compare projected and actual performance each month. Where there are large deviations, you must find out why and make whatever changes are necessary in your operations.

When I was the auditor for a small metallurgical firm a few years ago, I encountered a situation that is very common in new companies. During the early months of operation, the founder of the firm had prepared detailed budget forecasts. Then he put them in a drawer and never looked at them again. The firm did well from the beginning and showed a comfortable profit. After 18 months, with orders continuing to arrive in abundance, the company's molding equipment began to have increasing amounts of downtime because of repairs. With deadlines to meet, equipment was repaired only when it broke down. This situation became more and more frequent, and profitability began to decline. It was at this time that I was auditing the company's books. The founder dragged out his old projections and asked me to find out where he had underestimated his costs. I discovered that he had made no estimate of downtime in his projections, although he had included costs for preventive maintenance. When we discussed these old projections, he told me that no downtime was included with preventive maintenance estimates because such work "could be done at night." I found, however, that his actual maintenance costs were all for emergency repairs made during peak production periods. Business had grown so fast that he had neglected everything unrelated to immediate output, such as preventive maintenance. A comparison of his projected and actual monthly budgets would have brought this discrepancy to his attention, so he could have made changes in his operations and his budgets. Such changes, in turn, would have put his profit growth on a more stable footing. The use of financial controls enables you to evaluate your company's performance every month, to chart progress, and to compare anticipated with actual budgets. At the very least, a control system should give you the opportunity to deal with problems while there is still time to solve them.

A Final Word about Taxes

The federal and state governments will play an important role in your business. In return for maintaining the general level of the economy, such as it may be, paying unemployment insurance to the people you lay off, and monitoring the safety of your plant, they will request periodic fees in the form of sales tax, payroll tax, income tax, filing fees, and various other payments. I have therefore tried to outline below what some of your more important tax responsibilities will be at the time you start your firm.

The Employer's Federal Tax Responsibilities

1. Employer identification number. The company must submit a request in writing to its regional Internal Revenue Service center in order to obtain its identification number.

2. Federal income tax. The company is obligated to pay a tax on its taxable income, as defined. Usually, this tax amounts to 22 percent of the first $25,000 of taxable income and 48 percent of the balance.

3. F.I.C.A. tax. The company must match its employees' contributions to the F.I.C.A. (Social Security) fund.

4. Federal unemployment tax. The company's mandatory contribution to the federal unemployment fund is based on a certain percentage of its taxable payroll, as defined.

5. Employee tax withholdings. The employer must withhold federal income and F.I.C.A. taxes from its employees' wages in accordance with government-prepared tax tables. Failure to deposit these funds as required by law can result in penalties to the company as well as personal liability to the officers and/or directors of the company. This is one of the few instances where limited liability does not apply under the corporate structure.

The Employer's State Tax Responsibilities

1. Employer identification number. The states have requirements similar to federal requirements.

2. State income and franchise tax. The company must pay a certain percentage of its taxable income, as defined, to the state. Definitions of taxable income, applicable tax rates, and

so forth, vary considerably from state to state and are also affected by the state in which the company is incorporated, and whether or not the company is considered to be doing business in a given state.

3. State unemployment tax. The company must contribute a certain percentage of its taxable payroll, as defined, to the state unemployment fund. Rates and requirements vary from state to state.

4. State sales tax. Where applicable, the company will be required to file periodic reports and payments with the state. Rates and requirements vary from state to state.

5. Employee tax withholdings. State requirements are similar to federal requirements.

The foregoing are the basic tax obligations for all companies. Other obligations, federal and state excise taxes, property taxes, and so forth, should be investigated thoroughly before the beginning of business operations. The best sources of information concerning tax requirements are regional Internal Revenue Service centers, state tax headquarters, and your company's attorneys and accountants.

Exhibit 1

BALANCE SHEET FOR THE YEAR ENDED December 31,	1	2	3
ASSETS			
Current Assets			
Cash			15 000
Accounts Receivable			73 000
Inventory			82 000
Other current assets			11 000
TOTAL CURRENT ASSETS			181 000
Machinery and Equipment		25 000	
Less: Depreciation		6 000	
Net Machinery and Equipment		19 000	19 000
TOTAL ASSETS			200 000
LIABILITIES AND EQUITY			
Current Liabilities			
Accounts Payable			76 000
Notes Payable			2 000
Accrued Expenses			7 000
TOTAL CURRENT LIABILITIES			85 000
Long Term Debt			25 000
TOTAL LIABILITIES			110 000
Shareholders equity			
Common Stock			100 000
Retained Earnings (Losses)			(10 000)
TOTAL SHAREHOLDERS EQUITY			90 000
TOTAL LIABILITIES AND EQUITY			200 000

Exhibit 2

	November	December	December Yr. to Date	January Projection	
	1	2	3	4	5
PROFIT AND LOSS STATEMENT					
Sales	147 000	178 000	1 534 000	95 000	
Less Discounts and allowances	15 000	18 000	153 000	9 000	
NET SALES	132 000	160 000	1 381 000	86 000	
Cost of Sales					
Direct Labor	35 000	38 000	360 000	34 000	
Direct Materials	25 000	29 000	260 000	24 000	
Mfg. Overhead	10 000	12 000	110 000	9 000	
TOTAL COST OF Sls	70 000	79 000	730 000	67 000	
GROSS PROFIT	62 000	81 000	651 000	19 000	
Less:					
Mktng Expenses	9 000	11 000	92 000	5 000	
Exec Salaries	5 000	5 000	60 000	5 000	
Interest	1 000	1 000	12 000	1 000	
Computer Costs	1 000	1 000	12 000	1 000	
Professional Fees	500	500	6 000	500	
Depreciation	500	500	6 000	500	
Gen & Admin	2 000	2 000	24 000	2 000	
TOTAL OTHER EXP.	19 000	21 000	212 000	15 000	
Prov for Fed Tax	20 000	30 000	230 000	2 000	
NET PROFIT(LOSS)	23 000	30 000	209 000	2 000	

Exhibit 3

PROJECTED CASH FLOW FOR THE
MONTHS OF FEBRUARY AND MARCH

	February	March
Cash balance at beginning of Month	$ 19,000	$ 12,000
Cash Receipts		
Cash Sales	2,000	3,000
Collections from Accounts Receivable	65,000	74,000
Receipts from Insurance Payments	1,000	-
TOTAL CASH RECEIPTS	68,000	77,000
Cash Payments		
Payments for raw materials	43,000	41,000
Payments for wages	37,000	38,000
Expense payments	14,000	3,000
Payments for purchase of equipment	9,000	-
Payments for taxes	3,000	2,000
TOTAL CASH PAYMENTS	106,000	84,000
New Balance of Cash on Hand (required)	(19,000)	5,000
Transactions to obtain additional cash		
Obtained through Loans	31,000	-
Sale of marketable assets or securities	-	3,000
TOTAL NEW CASH	31,000	3,000
Cash balance carried to succeeding month	12,000	8,000

14 PRODUCTION

Bruce Backe*

This chapter treats the opportunities for success and the greater risks of failure in production planning rather than how to manufacture a product.

After spending most of my early days at IMLAC Corporation trying to figure out the most efficient way to manufacture computers in small quantities, I learned that success in manufacturing depends more on materials (production) control than on production methods. Certainly, methods are important; you must have reasonably efficient manufacturing processes. But while we were concentrating on this aspect, we got into serious trouble with available parts. We had a large inventory, but we didn't have everything that was needed when we needed it, and we had some things we didn't need. So, even with substantial investment capital committed to inventory, we were unable to ship units when we should have. Manufacturing methods could have been a lot less efficient at that stage, and it wouldn't have made much difference. Refinement of manufacturing techniques can be accomplished gradually without ill effects if you have a reasonable procedure to begin with. Design engineers can help you with this if necessary at the beginning. Unless you are in a business that

* Bruce Backe received his S.B. in management from M.I.T. He joined IMLAC Corporation as vice-president of operations, and is now president of that company.

depends on a breakthrough in manufacturing processes, don't make the usual mistake of putting more emphasis on methods than on *production* and *inventory control*. Production planning and decision making are what make or break most new businesses. Where there is no history to go on or extensive market research available, and where all other areas of your business are developing at the same time, a little more or less efficiency won't make much real difference.

In a new business, timing is the most important aspect of production planning. Having the product available in the right quantity at the right time seems simple enough, you may be thinking. But failure to do just this is one of the foremost causes of bankruptcy for new ventures. Sometimes resources are used to get the product ready for shipment before there are sufficient orders. With no revenues coming, the company runs out of money. On the other hand, not enough units may be ready when deliveries are due. Too many or too few units at critical times could spell disaster.

It would be a simple matter to calculate the appropriate product buildup if one could predict the rate of product development and sales progress. It would then only be necessary for the production planner to have the product available in the forecasted quantity. Product development and sales rarely proceed on schedule, however, making the production planning job more complex. The plan must accommodate as many variations as possible in the rate of engineering development and sales progress without a disastrous effect on capital. Furthermore, since lower product costs result from higher investment in capital equipment, the production planner is required to determine how much investment in capital equipment will give him a reasonably low product cost without putting him out of business if volume is less than expected.

At IMLAC both sales and development progress ran substantially behind plan (with sales being by far the worst), and since the opportunities to raise additional capital were essentially nonexistent (in 1970), we lived on the threshold of bankruptcy for two years. At first we committed far too many resources to production, although we didn't think so at the time. Fortunately, not too much of this investment was for capital equipment, so we were able to cut expenses drastically and in the nick of time until we were able to get more orders. From then on we were much more conservative in our production buildup, having had a good lesson in the vagaries of sales estimates. It's human nature to be interested in fantastic success stories (like Data General) and gradiose failures (like Viatron), but the best lessons probably come from more mundane, typical stories like ours. What finally enabled us to achieve success was the effort to avoid bankruptcy rather than an attempt to become an instantaneous giant. Today we are in a more solid position and are able to concentrate on growth.

At first glance, it might seem desirable for no production to start until engineering and product development are complete. What will the engineers do for a living once you start production? They may have to redesign the product because you can't make it the way they gave it to you in the first place. In production you will want to know if you can use a "widget" instead of a "whatsit" because you can't get "whatsits," and in any case you can't afford them. So the idea is to start working on those things before manufacturing costs build up, but not before the functional design looks reasonable, because you will find out where to get "whatsits" only to be told they aren't needed anyway. The "final" product will require engineering changes before and after being released to production in its ultimate form; thus a good part of the initial production effort is wasted. If this work has all been done on a conservative, low-key basis, the wasted effort will not be too costly compared to the progress. The engineering or product development staff will not be terminated upon completion of the original development work, and the cost of this organization *will* continue throughout the life of the business. Thus the advantage of having the product available to the market by starting some production prior to development completion will enable the company to produce revenues at an earlier stage than would otherwise be possible.

A good example of this at IMLAC was the development and production of power supplies for the PDS-1 Display Computer. In order to allow the small engineering staff to concentrate on the central processor design, we gave out a contract for the design and production of the power supplies as soon as the requirements could be established and long before we were in production on the main unit. This contract called for progress to be monitored by IMLAC during the design phase and a prototype approval to be issued before the supplier began any substantial production. The vendor had considerable problems along the way, and we were able to see that production of the power supply would not work the way we were doing it, with plenty of lead time before substantial quantities were needed and *without* having to spend any significant amount of money. Ultimately we built ten units in the house while getting the design bugs out and still satisfying early shipping requirements; then we had a number of assembly vendors bid on our final design for production quantities, getting them essentially when needed at a competitively low price and without having to raise our production payroll.

The relationship of production schedules to marketing and sales achievement is where the fun really begins. With all of the things that can go wrong along the way, it is a difficult enough job to produce something according to a given plan, but when the order forecast is off by orders of magnitude, pandemonium sets in. What usually happens first is that the sales forecast is glorious, and the production planner runs like hell to catch up. Because he is trying to go so fast to get the product ready when the orders start flowing, he incurs unnecessary cost and runs a grossly inefficient operation. He finally gets to the point where the product is ready to be delivered, only to find out that there are no orders—hence the word "layoff." Another possibility is that he is unable to build up fast enough to meet the actual order volume but still manages to incur substantial costs along the way. In this case, money is flowing out like crazy, with no revenues coming in because the product is not available for shipment. Either of these extremes can result in an early death. It is not unusual for the production manager who survives the first problem to become too conservative and be finished off by the second.

The Viatron example will illustrate my point. (In fact, IMLAC had a similar experience on a much smaller scale, so we were able to recover.) Revenues are committed to men and materials for production on a large scale consistent with sales dreams. In an attempt to "grow as rapidly as possible," substantial quantities of everything are acquired, but alas, in the confusion, certain details are overlooked or assumed to be unimportant. These minor details are such items as small parts believed to be readily available or the necessary quality to make the product really work in production as well as the handmade, spoon-fed prototype. Thus you have spent all your available capital on quantity but don't have a few complete and satisfactory units to ship. Most of the people I know (who are still in business) were fairly conservative players from the start. The fascinating thing is that the few really big successes were often achieved by the "go for broke" method, and of course you hear more about them. Unfortunately, it turns out to be the "go broke" method for most, and you hear of them only if they are able to get enough invested capital to do it in a spectacular way.

Let's assume that the first object is to stay alive, and the second is to grow profitably. (Most people state it the other

way around, but I have never been able to understand how
you can grow profitably if you are not alive.) Keeping this end
firmly in mind, the production planner can begin to see that
his job becomes one of playing percentages. He tries to develop
the production at a rate that will enable the company to stay
alive when the sales forecast turns out to be either optimistic or
pessimistic. It is surprising what a wide range of possibilities
can be accommodated with a little judicious planning. The
first step is to develop a steady rate of production, which can be
easily increased or decreased as the sales progress is measured.
It is wiser to start out with as low an investment in capital
equipment as the nature of the business will permit. By the
same token, it is desirable to have low-level commitments to
suppliers so that materials don't roll in the door when they are
not needed. Contracts can be written that will allow for *periodic
releases* of the necessary materials without excessive lead time.
You might have to make commitments for some material costs
to the supplier, but usually you can avoid a firm commitment
for the full amount particularly when you will allow some
rake-back pricing if you end up taking a lower quantity than
originally planned. This is generally better than just ordering
what is needed from time to time, because the supplier is
usually planning on a certain amount of production time for
you even if he hasn't actually started work.

If you didn't open this book directly to this page, you must
realize by now that there are more ways to fail in business than
there are to succeed. With this in mind, it is best to undertake
production planning with an approach geared to accommodate the most individual misadventures without bringing on
the ultimate ruination. As we began to utilize this approach at
IMLAC, we were able to avoid running out of funds even
though our estimates continued for some time afterward to be
very poor.

To facilitate production planning, prepare a graph showing

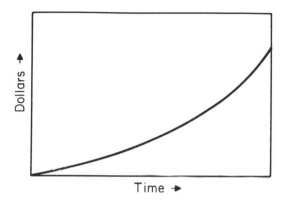

Figure 1. Single-line sales forecast

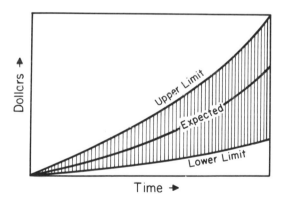

Figure 2. Variable-range sales forecast

projections for all major activities. Actual figures will vary from case to case, but the principles remain the same. Then—and this is *rarely* done—estimate the variations that are likely to occur. For example, your sales projection might look like Figure 1, but the most likely variations resemble Figure 2.

The object of your production planning is to accommodate the possible variations of the shaded area of Figure 2 rather than to prepare for the single-line forecast only. If the sales forecast has been perfectly accurate, you will make less profit, but the point is that you will make *some* profit at all levels if your production has been planned to take account of the variations. Of course, there is a limit to the range of possibilities that can be accommodated. But make the range as wide as possible at first, and then narrow it down as experience allows you to put things in sharper focus. You will give yourself a better chance to optimize profits without risking bankruptcy.

Figures 3 through 8 (at the end of this chapter) are simplified graphs that depict the relationships existing among cumulative operating costs, product costs, and revenues for a variety of hypothetical situations. For these examples, the following assumptions are made:

1. Cumulative operating costs include all costs incurred in operating a business and developing sales except the cost of manufacturing the product itself.
2. Invested cash starts out at $100 and cannot be replenished except by operating revenues.
3. Products can be turned immediately into cash upon receipt of an order if units are available for shipment.
4. The product becomes available in the period following production.
5. Unit production cost is $1 and unit selling price is $2.
6. Cumulative order volume is 55 units for the ten periods in Cases I and II and is 91 units for Case III. Each of the three cases has a different rate of accumulation to reach these total order volumes.

7. Operating costs remain the same in each case (that is, the production planner cannot accuse other departments of exceeding their budgets).

8. If the cash balance reaches zero, the entrepreneur is out of business (unless he can find a new source of financing and is willing to make major concessions).

The range of projected orders in Cases I, II, and III shown in Figure 3 covers the actual orders received shown in Figures 4 through 8. The production rate established in Figure 8 enables the company to operate successfully with any of the sales levels shown in the shaded area of Figure 3. If you study Figures 4 through 8, you can determine what happens when actual orders are less than projected or when the production rate is not adequate to meet the actual order rate.

Figure 4 represents a successful company start-up. Cash gets dangerously low in the eighth period but begins building up again after that. In this case, there is always sufficient product in inventory to meet incoming orders. By the eighth period, inventory reaches 21 units and remains at that level thereafter. The production rate is now exactly matched to orders. Although this may be fine for a product that must be sold from inventory, more cash could be made available for other purposes if the company were allowed to build up a backlog. For example, the company might want to invest in production equipment that would enable it to lower product costs.

In Figure 5, the production buildup (cumulative product costs) is the same as in Figure 4. But the rate of incoming orders is slower than expected. Even though the total number of orders received by the end of the tenth period is the same as in Figure 4, and is only five units lower in the eighth period, the high production rate leads to bankruptcy.

If the production planner had ordered a slower rate of buildup (cumulative product cost), such as that shown in Figure 6, he would have avoided bankruptcy, and the company would be in a modest backlog position by the end of the tenth period. In Figure 6, the incoming order rate is the same as for Figure 5. Note that this company could also fill the incoming orders shown in Figure 4. This buildup rate works in a number of situations. Since there is no way of knowing exactly what sales conditions will be, the plan that works successfully in most cases is, by definition, the best plan.

Of course, if your production buildup and concurrent costs are too low to meet incoming orders, your revenue rate will be too low for you to stay in business. This is shown in Figure 7. Here, the cash position reaches zero in the tenth period because there are not enough units to fill orders. (Remember that operating costs have not increased.)

In Figure 8, the production buildup is less than in Figure 4. The backlog does not get too high, since incoming orders are higher than anticipated. The actual production rate in Figure 8 is the same as in Figure 6. This now seems to be the best for the widest variety of conditions. In Figure 8, the cash flow is better than in any other situation, and a backlog of 42 units is produced by the end of the ninth period. It will not increase beyond that level (which represents a little over two months of production) if the 18-unit buildup rate is stabilized. The production planner who is confronted with the variations in sales shown in Figure 3 should establish the production rate shown in Figure 8. He will then be able to accommodate all sales possibilities without going bankrupt. He will also be prepared to optimize profits for the rate actually achieved.

It can be seen that little harm is done if the production rate is relatively conservative. More often than not, a company that starts out with adequate capital spends itself into oblivion because it is not in a position to ship against profitable orders because of either inadequate sales or unavailability of product. There are, of course, many possible variations beyond those shown. The figures are meant only to demonstrate that even seemingly minor variations in timing can have a disastrous result (such as the differences between Figures 4 and 5 or between Figures 6 and 7). In actual practice, the variations are often more extreme. One could, of course, increase the marketing budget, and consequently operating costs, in the hope of creating higher sales volume. This could prove to be more profitable in the long run but must always remain within the resources available, and the risk becomes progressively greater as resources are more rapidly used.

These curves concentrate on the success or failure of the business due to running out of cash. Once the business has remained alive, the next step is to maximize the profit. Again, timing plays a major part. Investment in capital equipment which will lower product cost and increase profits is often desirable once it is clear that the sales volume being attained will support the investment in equipment. The profit will end up being the greatest if all of the various aspects of the business can be brought into harmony.

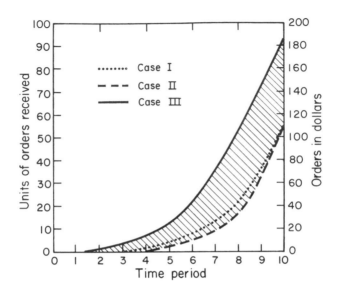

Figure 3. Variable-range sales forecast (orders received)

	Time period									
	1	2	3	4	5	6	7	8	9	10
Three cases with different levels of assumed orders received										
Case I: Figure 4	0	0	0	1	2	3	6	7	18	18
Case II: Figures 5, 6, 7	0	0	0	0	1	3	4	6	18	23
Case III: Figure 8	0	1	2	3	6	7	18	18	18	18
Cumulative units										
Case I: Figure 4	0	0	0	1	3	6	12	19	37	55
Case II: Figures 5, 6, 7	0	0	0	0	1	4	8	14	32	55
Case III: Figure 8	0	1	3	6	12	17	37	55	73	91
Orders in dollars = $2 × number of units ordered (Assumption 5)										

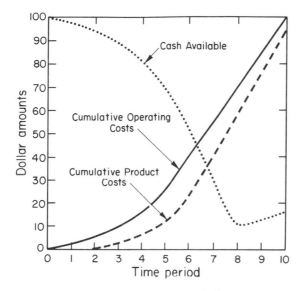

Figure 4. Inventory position maintained

	Time period									
	1	2	3	4	5	6	7	8	9	10
Orders received (Case I)	0	0	0	1	2	3	6	7	18	18
Product available	0	0	0	2	5	9	16	28	39	39
Product shipped	0	0	0	1	2	3	6	7	18	18
Ending inventory	0	0	0	1	3	6	10	21	21	21
Ending backlog	0	0	0	0	0	0	0	0	0	0

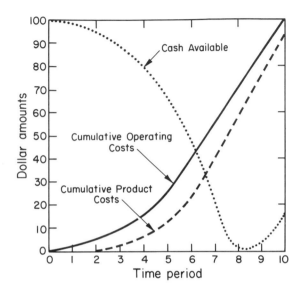

Figure 5. Production too fast for orders. Company goes bankrupt in eighth period.

	Time period									
	1	2	3	4	5	6	7	8	9	10
Orders received (Case II)	0	0	0	0	1	3	4	6	18	23
Product available	0	0	0	2	6	11	18	32	44	44
Product shipped	0	0	0	0	1	3	4	6	18	23
Ending inventory	0	0	0	2	5	8	14	26	26	21
Ending backlog	0	0	0	0	0	0	0	0	0	0

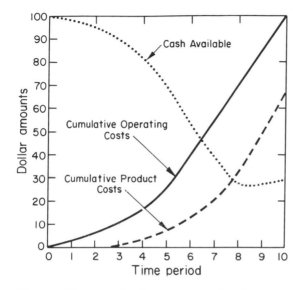

Figure 6. Slower production rate creates backlog and saves company.

	Time period									
	1	2	3	4	5	6	7	8	9	10
Orders received (Case II)	0	0	0	0	1	3	4	6	18	23
Product available	0	0	0	1	3	6	9	13	17	18
Product shipped	0	0	0	0	1	3	4	6	17	18
Ending inventory	0	0	0	1	2	3	5	7	0	0
Ending backlog	0	0	0	0	0	0	0	0	1	6

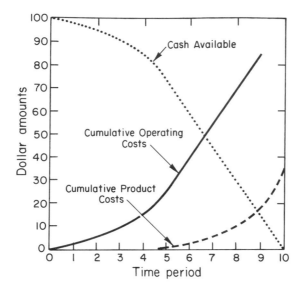

Figure 7. Too slow a production rate causes bankruptcy in tenth period.

	Time period									
	1	2	3	4	5	6	7	8	9	10
Orders received (Case II)	0	0	0	0	1	3	4	6	18	23
Product available	0	0	0	0	0	1	2	3	4	8
Product shipped	0	0	0	0	0	1	2	3	4	8
Ending inventory	0	0	0	0	0	0	0	0	0	0
Ending backlog	0	0	0	0	1	1	3	6	20	35

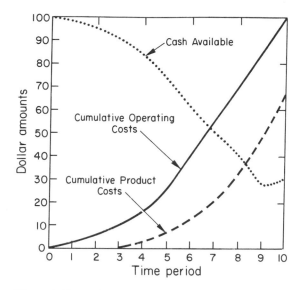

Figure 8. Strong backlog position

	Time period									
	1	2	3	4	5	6	7	8	9	10
Orders received (Case III)	0	1	2	3	6	7	18	18	18	18
Product available	0	0	0	1	2	4	6	8	10	18
Product shipped	0	0	0	1	2	4	6	8	10	18
Ending inventory	0	0	0	0	0	0	0	0	0	0
Ending backlog	0	1	3	5	9	12	24	34	42	42

15 CONSULTING SERVICES

Julian J. Bussgang*

Many Americans, and indeed people everywhere, dream of going into business for themselves. The easiest business to begin is one involving personal services because it requires fewer facilities and the least capitalization. In this chapter I shall consider certain aspects of developing a technical services business, with the major emphasis on personal services. I shall discuss the policies that can lead to success and the dollars-and-cents issue of pricing a personal service.

Key Policies

Success in the services business means always running fully booked. To reach that stage, you must establish certain key policies. These include availability, fair pricing, proper personnel assignments, and adequate company size. Above all, you must seek to establish and maintain a reputation for high-quality service and dependability.

Availability
If a customer needs a service on short notice, it must be part of your policy to supply it. You cannot play hard to get and

* Julian J. Bussgang received his B.Sc. degree from the University of London, his S.M. degree in electrical engineering from M.I.T., and his Ph.D. in applied physics from Harvard University. In 1962 he founded Signatron, Inc., a research and development consulting company, of which he is currently the president.

expect another call. Customers must learn to depend on you whenever they need your services. Otherwise, they will search elsewhere for new sources. An additional job can frequently be squeezed in when you come to realize that the urgency of the project is frequently overstated by the customer. Sometimes the client who tells you that he wants to begin "immediately" will not be able to get his organization's approval to start the job until months later. Nevertheless, it always pays to extend yourself since no business can really grow without some overload. It also pays to have some personnel prospects on tap to react rapidly to new opportunities.

Fair Pricing

You should not take advantage of a customer's desperate need for your services. If you do so, you may lose in the long run. The customer must learn that if he turns to you when he is in a bind, he will not be held up. The fair-pricing policy can be likened to becoming a competitively priced supermarket with a steady flow of all-week shoppers pushing fully loaded carts rather than a high-priced weekend grocery store catering to occasional single-item customers in distress.

Proper Personnel Assignments

Your people should be competent and properly classified with regard to fees and capabilities. The question of assignments requires a full understanding of the proposed project before it begins. If junior men are assigned to work away from your company office, a senior member of the firm should be in frequent contact with the client and with your own staff on the job to counsel and to monitor. You must be alert to the necessity of changing personnel or lending a hand when things are not going well. You should also look for opportunities to supply additional time and personnel as you become acquainted with other problems of the client.

Adequate Size

The size of the staff is a significant factor in the success of the personal services business. Adequate size is essential because it permits availability, a variety of talents, and maximum exposure, which will inspire confidence in your organization. Many overload jobs require large teams or teams with diverse skills. This is particularly true when there is a surplus of technical personnel on the labor market. Any potential customer can hire one programmer, one engineer, or one technician when he needs a little additional help. But it is a different story when a department store needs ten programmers to install a new accounting system or when an electronics company needs a temporary team of two mechanical engineers and three electrical engineers to fulfill some unusual requirement for a rush contract. Studies of how clients choose personal services companies show that the size of a service organization is frequently a critical factor in its selection. The larger the consulting service, the better its chances of getting an unsolicited job from a first-time client. A new operation is, of course, likely to be very small. In order to inspire confidence, you can compensate by indicating that you or your associates have worked with companies of adequate size. Sometimes a small new company has a depth of talent in one specific area. This is reassuring to the prospective client. I disagree with the entrepreneurs who begin a business determined to keep it small. This may be a legitimate decision, but I question the notion that a services business must be small to be manageable and to maintain quality. I believe that you are handicapping your business unnecessarily if you do not set growth as one of your primary goals. Static companies in any business can have trouble retaining their young personnel.

Reputation

Attaining a good reputation in your business area of course must be one of the key policies. In other words, your company must achieve recognition for the quality of the services it supplies. You must have a good record for services performed and appropriate publicity to make your services and company name well known to prospective customers. Public relations and advertising are especially crucial if there is little distinction between your company's capabilities and those of your competitors. This is a well-established principle in selling soap, and it applies just as firmly to services. Proper promotion is a matter of good taste and should be scaled to your achievements and resources. It never paid anybody to advertise goods that were not on the shelf.

Pricing the Service

The first question asked by entrepreneurs starting a personal technical services business is "How much should we charge for our time?" Begin with the salary you want to draw from the business. Suppose that salary is $15,600. As an employee you have this figure prorated to $1300 a month, $300 a week, $60 a day, or $7.50 an hour—however you want to state it. A business pays employees at these rates but has to charge higher rates to cover expenses and time spent in the normal course of business that cannot be charged to customers. Each of us knows an individual consultant who bills for 60 hours a week. Maybe that kind of effort is occasionally possible, but few people have the capacity or desire to work more than 48 hours a week as a steady diet. Even the hardiest souls are occasionally sick, take holidays, attend weddings, or pass papers on a new house. Thus, although the nominal annual working time may be 40 times 52, or 2080 hours, the actual hours available to charge to customers are fewer. Table 1 gives a sample calculation.

The remaining 1872 hours represent 36 hours a week for 52 weeks. In addition, you should allow one day a week (52 days a year) for marketing, proposal writing, calls on customers,

Table 1

Vacations (2 weeks)	80 hours
Holidays (9 days)	72 hours
(New Year's Day, Washington's Birthday, Memorial Day, Independence Day, Labor Day, Veterans' Day, Thanksgiving, day after Thanksgiving, Christmas)	
Sick and personal time (average 5 days)	40 hours
Snow days (2 days)	16 hours
Total unavailable hours	208 hours

Table 2

Secretarial	$1200
Office space	750
Payroll taxes	600
Insurance (personal and business)	500
Telephone	300
Supplies and duplicating services	300
Miscellaneous (travel, legal, auditing, subscriptions, and other)	250
Total	$3900

attendance at meetings, correspondence, office routines, professional and other necessary activities. This brings you to an average of 28 hours a week that are available to charge to customers in the course of one year. Now, no motel runs at an occupancy rate of 100 percent, and no service business can operate at 100 percent capacity either. You should allow about 10 percent of your available time for load fluctuations, unpaid courtesy service, and so forth. From this calculation it becomes evident that 25 hours a week of customer charges may have to carry the full 40-hour salary plus other overhead expenses. These 25 hours are called the "direct" labor hours. The remaining 15 hours are called "indirect" labor hours.

Other overhead expenses vary from business to business. Table 2 gives an example of "other" overhead expenses per employee per year.

Though space requirements for each business are different—one needs a basement, another a suite of offices—the impact of these differences on total overhead is not as large as might be expected. This is so because indirect labor and other expenses common to all businesses (such as payroll taxes) tend to dominate overhead costs. The representative figure of $3900 in other overhead expenses per man-year is $75 per man per week. This means that, for our $15,000 a year consultant, the 25 hours directly charged to customer accounts per week must carry the $300 a week for salary plus $75 a week in other expenses.

Finally, the new company must plan on making some profit. A reasonable pretax profit factor to aim for in a strictly personal services business is 12 percent. This translates into a charge of $375 × 1.12 = $420 for the 25 direct hours (that is, $16.80 an hour or $134.40 a day) in order to generate the desired salary of $7.50 an hour ($60 a day). The multiplier on the salary is thus 2.24, representing 100 percent overhead and 12 percent fee.

What happens when the base salary is lower? The other overhead expenses will be larger in proportion to the salary expense, and the employee is less likely to spend time selling. When the base salary is higher, the other overhead expenses are less, relative to the salary, but the employee is more likely to spend time selling, carrying out administrative tasks, participating in professional activities, and so forth. Thus these two components of overhead cost tend to balance each other to produce a relatively constant multiplier regardless of the salary level.

Our $15,600 salary figure and the 2.24 multiplier are actually rather low for most businesses that sell services. Well-established companies that have specialized knowledge, established reputations, and investments in their own research or proprietary data base are more likely to operate with multipliers in the 2.5 to 3.0 range. The higher multiplier is important if your customers demand many conferences before the work begins and a great deal of follow-up after it ends. Remember that it is in the customer's interest to be dealing with a company that makes a profit and markets its services. Thus it is in the customer's interest to pay a fair price for the cost of services. A supplier who makes no profit and does not market his services will not survive. The customer looking for bargains ends up dealing with suppliers who are in and out of the bankruptcy courts. Naturally, such suppliers will not be able to complete their work, add to it, or improve it. In my experience, the client who understands something about business operations seeks fair prices but does not hunt for bargains. The bargain hunter should be considered suspect—someone who really does not need the service, cannot afford it, or will not pay.

The most frustrating problem encountered by a company selling time to an inexperienced customer is explaining why you must charge $16.80 an hour for the services of an employee making $7.50 an hour. An inexperienced client may assume that the employee is making $35,000 a year rather than $15,600, or that the company is making excessive profits. The truth is that the customer's company would incur all the expenses incurred by the services company (except perhaps marketing and profit) if the same man were on his payroll. In fact, the employee's idle time would probably be greater. He might relax a little longer in the company cafeteria or lounge. There would be more administrative expense as well, plus recruiting and training costs. Once hired, the employee would have to sell himself to other departments of his organization to justify his continuing presence on the payroll. So even the marketing expense would not be avoided altogether.

Despite this rationale for a realistic price structure, which means a multiplier of 2.24, you will find yourself under pressure to cut prices in order to get started. This is just not a wise maneuver, however. In the first place, the costs of starting a new enterprise are greater because of the initial sales effort and start-up expenses that are unavoidable. There is an even more compelling reason to establish a fair price structure immediately: customers do not like rate fluctuations. An artificially low rate would force you to make upward adjustments soon after the business got going. In some government contracts, the contractor is required to certify that his rates are no higher than what he has been charging on other occasions for the same service. Under these conditions, it is difficult to move rates up and down like a commodities market. It is also unfair to charge one customer one rate and another customer a different rate. It would be downright embarrassing if the two customers were to compare notes. Thus, although certain types of service (night or weekend work, short-notice jobs, out-of-town trips, court appearances) may require a higher rate, there are strong reasons to apply a reasonable fixed rate to all customers across the board. A college professor who consults occasionally to supplement his income may quote rates as the spirit moves him: one rate if he is busy, another if he has a vacation. But a professional service company must have an established price structure for the time it sells, or the enterprise will not last. Fair prices are not a handicap in business development. Quality and appropriateness of services are much more important than price. Satisfied customers always pay first. Dissatisfied customers pay last and argue about prices. You can avoid having your prices questioned by establishing good communications with your customers before and during the jobs you perform for them.

The concept of starting one's own business is part of the spirit of America. There is no individual of whom we should be prouder than the one who is willing to take the risk and, with faith in his own unique abilities, to start a new venture. It sets him apart, as it has set our country apart.

Sometimes, because we become accustomed to those things we have known from childhood, we forget that General Motors, du Pont, and IBM were each started by one person. When an entrepreneur cuts his ties with job security to begin a new venture, the professionals with whom he deals—whether attorneys, accountants, or bankers—never really know if they are witnessing the birth of greatness. In fact, the haunting but unspoken fear of missing this year's "Xerox" drives us all to make judgments and to take risks that perhaps we should not take.

The support of an entrepreneur should be for positive reasons, however, for he is the one who enhances competition, increases the production of goods and services, and increases the velocity of money. He creates jobs for the community and raises its productivity, thus enabling men to increase their standard of living.

Of course, accolades for the entrepreneur must be tempered with words of caution. John Greenleaf Whittier, the Quaker poet, said that the saddest words of tongue or pen are "It might have been!" In the entrepreneurial field, the saddest words are not "It might have been" but "the limitations of originators." They often come from large institutions, which they leave, perhaps unwittingly, because they do not fit in a large institution. Five or ten years later, if successful, they are the leaders of their own large organization, and sometimes that is not their psychological place. Sadly, their lack of qualification for management of a large company requires that they be pushed aside, often with some pain. The possibility of such an event of course should never deter the entrepreneur or his backers. It is helpful, however, if he has some understanding of this eventuality, and with that understanding he may avoid it.

Therefore, let no entrepreneur hesitate when he understands his ability to create the unique. Let all of us stand behind him and say, "Another entrepreneur—God bless him!"

Arthur F. F. Snyder
President, Bank of the Commonwealth
Detroit, Michigan

BIBLIOGRAPHY

Allen, Louis L. *Starting and Succeeding in Your Own Small Business.* New York: Grosset & Dunlap, 1968.

Anthony, Robert N. *Management Accounting.* Homewood, Ill: Richard D. Irwin, 1964.

"Bill Lear and His New Engine." *Forbes*, Vol. 107, No. 3 (Feb. 1, 1971), p. 36.

Broom, H. N., and J. G. Longnecker. *Small Business Management.* 2nd ed. Cincinnati: South-Western Publishing Company, 1966.

Bylinsky, Gene. "General Doriot's Dream Factory." *Fortune*, Vol. 76, No. 2 (Aug. 1967), pp. 103–107.

Center for Venture Management. *The Entrepreneur and New Enterprise Formation: A Bibliography.* Milwaukee: Center for Venture Management, 1970.

Dible, Donald M. *Up Your Own Organization.* Palo Alto, Calif.: Entrepreneur Press, 1972.

Fortune magazine, ed. *Adventures in Small Business.* New York: McGraw-Hill Book Company, 1957.

Gross, Harry. *Financing for Small and Medium-Sized Businesses.* Englewood Cliffs, N.J.: Prentice-Hall, 1969.

Herbert, Evan. "How a Young Company Changes." *Innovation*, No. 12 (1970), pp. 12–25.

Hutchinson, G. Scott, ed. *The Business of Acquisitions and Mergers.* New York: Presidents Publishing House, 1968.

Hutchinson, G. Scott, ed. *Why, When, and How to Go Public.* New York: Presidents Publishing House, 1970.

Kelley, Pearce C., Kenneth Lawyer, and Clifford M. Baumback. *How to Organize and Operate a Small Business.* 4th ed. Englewood Cliffs, N.J.: Prentice-Hall, 1968.

Leavitt, Harold J. *Managerial Psychology.* Chicago: University of Chicago Press, 1964.

"Letter Stock Is Worth the Worry." *Business Week*, No. 2055 (Jan. 18, 1969), pp. 108–114.

Novotny, Carl H., and David S. Searles, Jr. *Venture Capital in the United States: An Analysis.* Chestnut Hill, Mass.: New Enterprise Systems, 1970. Available from New Enterprise Systems, P.O. Box 61, 850 Boylston St., Chestnut Hill, Mass. 02167.

Peters, Donald H. "The Development of Frozen Orange Juice Concentrate." *Research Management*, Vol. 11, No. 1 (Jan, 1968), pp. 45–60.

Roberts, Edward B. "Entrepreneurship and Technology." *Research Management*, Vol. 11, No. 4 (July, 1968), pp. 249–266.

Roberts, Edward B. "How to Succeed in a New Technology Enterprise." *Technology Review*, Vol. 73, No. 2 (Dec., 1970), pp. 22–27.

Steinmetz, Laurence L., John B. Kline, and Donald P. Stegall. *Managing the Small Business.* Homewood, Ill.: Richard D. Irwin, 1968.

Technimetrics, Inc. *Venture Capital.* New York: Technimetrics, 1970. Available from Technimetrics, 527 Madison Avenue, New York, N.Y. 10022.

U.S. Congress, Senate, Document No. 91-45. Senate Select Committee on Small Business and House Select Committee on Small Business, 91st Cong., 1st Sess. *Handbook for Small Business.* 3rd ed. Washington, D.C.: U.S. Government Printing Office, 1969.

U.S. Small Business Administration. *A Survey of Federal Government Publications of Interest to Small Business.* 3rd ed. Washington, D.C.: U.S. Government Printing Office, 1969.

"Venture Capital in a Bear Market." *Forbes,* Vol. 105, No. 12 (June 15, 1970), pp. 28–37.

INDEX